TERRORISM

DATE DUE

SEP			
SEP 27 2007			

TERRORISM

GREAT SPEECHES IN HISTORY

Debra A. Miller,
Book Editor

Daniel Leone, *President*

Bonnie Szumski, *Publisher*

Scott Barbour, *Managing Editor*

GREENHAVEN
PRESS®

GALE

San Diego • Detroit • New York • San Francisco • Cleveland
New Haven, Conn. • Waterville, Maine • London • Munich

© 2003 by Greenhaven Press. Greenhaven Press is an imprint of The Gale Group, Inc., a division of Thomson Learning, Inc.

Greenhaven® and Thomson Learning™ are trademarks used herein under license.

For more information, contact
Greenhaven Press
27500 Drake Rd.
Farmington Hills, MI 48331-3535
Or you can visit our Internet site at http://www.gale.com

Cover credit: © Associated Press, AP

LIBRARY OF CONGRESS CATALOGING-IN-PUBLICATION DATA

Terrorism / Debra A. Miller, book editor.
   p. cm. — (Greenhaven Press's great speeches in history)
Includes bibliographical references and index.
ISBN 0-7377-1872-2 (lib. : alk. paper) — ISBN 0-7377-1873-0 (pbk. : alk. paper)
   1. Terrorism—History—Sources. 2. Speeches, addresses, etc. I. Miller, Debra A.
II. Great speeches in history series
HV6431.T4635 2003
303.6'25'09—dc21
                                                    2002192794

Printed in the United States of America

Contents

year 2002, even after the signing of a power-sharing peace agreement that many thought would end the conflict there, British prime minister Tony Blair called on the IRA to end its paramilitary activity in order to achieve lasting peace.

Chapter 4: Islamic Fundamentalist Terrorism and September 11, 2001

attacks against U.S. targets as well as threats from countries like Iraq and Iran involving weapons of mass destruction.

Foreword

I have a dream that one day this nation will rise up and live out the true meaning of its creed: "We hold these truths to be self-evident: that all men are created equal."

I have a dream that one day on the red hills of Georgia the sons of former slaves and the sons of former slave owners will be able to sit down together at the table of brotherhood.

I have a dream that one day even the state of Mississippi, a state sweltering with the heat of injustice, sweltering with the heat of oppression, will be transformed into an oasis of freedom and justice.

I have a dream that my four little children will one day live in a nation where they will not be judged by the color of their skin but by the content of their character.

Perhaps no speech in American history resonates as deeply as Martin Luther King Jr.'s "I Have a Dream," delivered in 1963 before a rapt audience of 250,000 on the steps of the Lincoln Memorial in Washington, D.C. Decades later, the speech still enthralls those who read or hear it, and stands as a philosophical guidepost for contemporary discourse on racism.

What distinguishes "I Have a Dream" from the hundreds of other speeches given during the civil rights era are King's eloquence, lyricism, and use of vivid metaphors to convey abstract ideas. Moreover, "I Have a Dream" serves not only as a record of history—a testimony to the racism that permeated American society during the 1960s—but it is also a historical event in its own right. King's speech, aired live on national television, marked the first time that the grave injustice of racism was fully articulated to a mass audience in a way that was both logical and evocative. Julian Bond, a fellow participant in the civil rights movement and student of King's, states that

> King's dramatic 1963 "I Have a Dream" speech before the Lincoln Memorial cemented his place as first among equals in civil rights leadership; from this first televised mass meeting, an American audience saw and heard the unedited oratory of America's finest preacher, and for the first time, a mass white audience heard the undeniable justice of black demands.

Moreover, by helping people to understand the justice of the civil rights movement's demands, King's speech helped to transform the nation. In 1964, a year after the speech was delivered, President Lyndon B. Johnson signed the Civil Rights Act, which outlawed segregation in public facilities and discrimination in employment. In 1965, Congress passed the Voting Rights Act, which forbids restrictions, such as literacy tests, that were commonly used in the South to prevent blacks from voting. King's impact on the country's laws illustrates the power of speech to bring about real change.

Greenhaven Press's Great Speeches in History series offers students an opportunity to read and study some of the greatest speeches ever delivered before an audience. Each volume traces a specific historical era, event, or theme through speeches—both famous and lesser known. An introductory essay sets the stage by presenting background and context. Then a collection of speeches follows, grouped in chapters based on chronology or theme. Each selection is preceded by a brief introduction that offers historical context, biographical information about the speaker, and analysis of the speech. A comprehensive index and an annotated table of contents help readers quickly locate material of interest, and a bibliography serves as a launching point for further research. Finally, an appendix of author biographies provides detailed background on each speaker's life and work. Taken together, the volumes in the Greenhaven Great Speeches in History series offer students vibrant illustrations of history and demonstrate the potency of the spoken word. By reading speeches in their historical context, students will be transported back in time and gain a deeper understanding of the issues that confronted people of the past.

Introduction

On September 11, 2001, America witnessed firsthand the dangers of modern terrorism. On that date terrorists armed with box cutters hijacked commercial airplanes and flew them into the two World Trade Center towers in New York City and into the Pentagon in Washington, D.C., killing thousands. A fourth hijacked airplane crashed in Pennsylvania on its way toward Washington, D.C., killing all passengers. To many Americans these attacks seemed to come out of nowhere, for no reason. Eventually, Americans learned that al-Qaeda, an extremist Islamic terrorist group based in Afghanistan, and its leader, Osama bin Laden, were to blame. Al-Qaeda was the same terrorist group that was responsible for several other attacks on Americans in recent years. These included a 1993 bomb explosion at the World Trade Center that caused 6 deaths and numerous injuries; a 1998 bomb attack on U.S. embassies in Kenya and Tanzania that killed 224 (12 of them Americans); and a 2000 attack in Yemen on the American destroyer the USS *Cole* that killed 17 sailors and wounded 30. September 11, however, was different—this terror struck at home killing large numbers of people, and Americans watched the horror live on national television.

After the September 11 attacks, U.S. president George Bush declared "war on terrorism." To date, this war has involved a U.S. attack on and defeat of the Taliban regime in Afghanistan (which gave sanctuary to al-Qaeda); the destruction of al-Qaeda's bases in that country; a worldwide, ongoing effort by the United States and other concerned countries to hunt down and destroy al-Qaeda and its leaders; and many other systemic measures designed to prevent terrorism and improve cooperation among countries fighting terror.

In January 2002 President Bush warned of another facet of terrorism—an "axis of evil," referring to countries such as Iraq, Iran, and North Korea, which he says sponsor terrorism and seek to develop chemical, biological, and nuclear weapons. Soon thereafter, President Bush threatened war with Iraq, arguing that Saddam Hussein's regime must be removed because it continues to develop weapons of mass destruction that could be supplied to terrorists or used against the United States or its allies. The president called on the United Nations (UN) for help, leading to a renewal of UN weapons inspections in Iraq (inspectors in the 1990s monitored Iraq's compliance with UN disarmament requirements stemming from Iraq's invasion of Kuwait in 1990) and possibly to military action against that country if it resists the inspections process or evidence shows it has failed to disarm. In October 2002 North Korea admitted to U.S. diplomats that it was developing nuclear weapons in violation of a 1994 agreement with the United States. This posed yet another serious threat of terrorism, but one which the Bush administration hoped to resolve through diplomacy.

Given the nation's new focus on terrorism, many seek to understand why America is targeted, why innocent civilians are being killed, and what possible reason exists for such terrorist violence. The truth is that terrorism has existed throughout human history in one form or another. However, in the past more "traditional" terrorists have mostly targeted noncivilians, sought to limit the number of their victims, and often justified their use of violence based on specific political or economic goals. Such goals have included revolution against tyranny or unjust governments, political independence for a particular people, or opposition to specific government policies. In some cases such terrorist groups have been neutralized through strategies of negotiation and involvement in democratic processes—that is, by seeking political solutions.

Al-Qaeda and similar modern religious terrorists are different, and potentially much more dangerous, than many past terrorists. This is because they specifically target civilians, seek the notoriety of killing large numbers of people, and have access to modern weapons and technology—and possibly to weapons of mass destruction. In addition, these terrorists appear to be motivated more by religious fervor than specific political goals. Al-Qaeda and similar groups express a general opposition to all American and Western involvement in the Middle East (such as the presence of U.S. troops stationed in Saudi Arabia following Iraq's invasion of Kuwait), loathing for moderate Arab governments aligned with the United States, and support for Arab causes such as the Palestinian opposition to Israel. However, the main goal of radical Islamic groups appears to be a jihad, or Islamic holy war, against the West, the spread of their fundamentalist religious beliefs, and the creation of Islamic religious states in the Middle East similar to Iran's Islamic Revolution or the Taliban regime that controlled Afghanistan in the late 1990s. Due to their religious aspirations and willingness to kill civilians, modern terrorists are much more destructive than terrorists of the past. It is also more difficult to devise political or nonmilitary options for defending against such terrorism.

Defining Terrorism

The first question that arises in any study of terrorism is how to define it. Although many definitions have been offered by scholars, most definitions include: (1) the use of violence, (2) for the purpose of inspiring terror in the larger population, (3) by persons or groups who do not possess the resources or popular support to fight the enemy through a direct military assault. Also, terrorists typically yearn for media publicity to spread news of their acts.

Problems arise with any definition, however, because of the wide range of types, uses, and perpetrators of terrorism. Terror has been used for both noble and ignoble causes, and by private groups as well as by states. For example, it has been employed by revolutionaries in France and Russia seeking to overthrow unjust governments, by native peoples in Algeria and Libya to rebel against colonial monarchies, and by cruel state dictators such as Hitler and Stalin to eliminate opposition and oppress or destroy entire populations. Terror

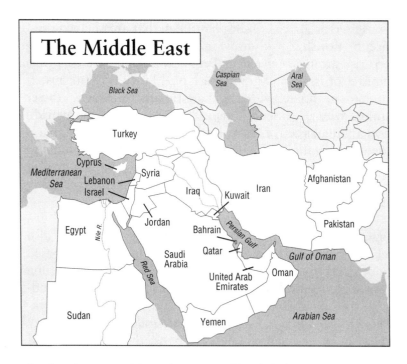

The Middle East

also has been used by advocates of both left-wing and right-wing beliefs. The United States itself has seen both left-wing domestic terrorists, such as the Black Panthers, who fought against racial oppression and discrimination in the 1960s, and right-wing terror, such as the 1995 bombing in Oklahoma City by Timothy McVeigh, a gun enthusiast and right-wing conservative angry at the federal government.

Further, whether a terror campaign is viewed as a legitimate struggle against injustice or as evil often depends on one's political perspective and bias. Groups labeled as terrorists often refer to themselves not as terrorists but as "freedom fighters." This term reflects their strong belief that their cause is honorable and that their use of violence or terror is justified, much the same way governments justify the use of military violence in defense of a strategic goal. Indeed, an examination of history suggests that in some cases a cause initially viewed as terrorist by most of the world later becomes accepted as a legitimate political goal once the terrorist group acquires popular support and a legitimate political power base. For example, Israel was granted nationhood only after

Jewish terror attacks on British rule in that area helped pressure the British to withdraw; indeed, the leader of the Jewish terrorist group, Menachem Begin, was later elected prime minister of Israel and granted a Nobel Peace Prize for his efforts to negotiate with the Palestinians. Similarly, Yasser Arafat, who developed a reputation as one of the world's most infamous terrorists as leader of the Palestinian Liberation Organization (PLO), later moved toward diplomacy, was elected as legitimate leader of the Palestinian-controlled areas, and was also awarded a Nobel Peace Prize for his negotiating efforts.

Because of the difficulties in defining terrorism and distinguishing it from legitimate political struggles, there is also debate about the best way to respond to it. One view, based on evidence that much of the world's terrorism has sprung from some form of oppression, is that it is important to address the underlying injustices that give rise to the desperation evidenced in terrorist acts. France followed this strategy when native Algerians rose up to oppose the French colonial rule; Algeria was awarded its independence, ending the civil war initiated by terror strikes there.

Others point out that this strategy does not always work. In Spain, for example, after the dictator Francisco Franco oppressed the local Basque population leading to terrorist demands for Basque independence, the country adopted democratic rule and granted greater autonomy to the Basque people. Though this satisfied both the vast majority of Basques and Spaniards, a small minority of Basque terrorists still fight on years later, demanding complete independence.

Those opposing appeasement and negotiation with terrorists argue that it is necessary to simply eradicate the terrorist threat through strong government or military responses to terrorist acts. The nature of terrorism, however, allows it to be waged by a very small group with few resources. Thus, it is often very difficult to completely destroy terrorism; instead, the effort becomes one of constant vigilance over a long period of time. Sometimes, too, the very act of strongly cracking down on terrorism can inspire and win popular support for the terrorists' cause. This occurred in Ireland when the British responded viciously to early struggles for Irish independence, creating Irish martyrs, voter support for the rebels, and an eventual treaty with the so-called terrorists that created an independent Irish state.

Today's religious terrorists pose a particularly perplexing problem for those seeking solutions to terror. Terrorists such as these, motivated increasingly by religious rather than political goals, negate the opportunity for political solutions and thus perhaps narrow the options for nonmilitary responses. If the issue is one of secularism versus religious rule in the Muslim world, and if the terrorists' fight is essentially a holy war seeking to eradicate all secular and Western influences from the Middle East, there is little room for political compromise. The United States is unlikely to simply abandon all its strategic interests in the Middle East, particularly its interests in oil access, in order to pacify al-Qaeda. Nor is the Western world likely to allow destruction of the state of Israel, the goal of some radical Islamic groups fighting for the Palestinian cause. The battle against Islamic terror thus becomes a war of attrition in which terrorists have the benefit of a seemingly constant supply of new Muslim recruits. It is ultimately a war for the hearts and minds of the millions of Muslims throughout the world. They must choose between the brand of fundamentalist, revolutionary, and anti-Western Islam advocated by al-Qaeda and a more moderate Islam that allows for modern, secular governments and friendly relations with Western countries such as the United States.

Traditional Terrorism Throughout History

A historical view of terrorism reveals, with few exceptions, a pattern driven largely by political motives, targeting mostly governmental figures or sites, and using conventional weapons in mostly conventional ways. In addition, except for state-run terror campaigns, historically most terrorist groups have caused only a limited number of casualties, seeking publicity for their cause with the least amount of violence necessary. Typically, past groups have also been highly organized and run like military operations from specific geographical locations.

Examples of political motives for terror occurred as early as the eighteenth century in the French Revolution. During the reign of King Louis XVI and his queen, Marie Antoinette, in 1789 the peasants and others rebelled, seeking democratic and economic reforms. The king and queen were removed from the throne and eventually executed, and a new revolutionary government was created to take control of France. The revolutionaries, led by Maximilien Robespierre, launched a broad Reign of Terror (as it was later called) aimed at eliminating all opposition to the revolution. Tens of thousands who were labeled as threats to the revolution died by guillotine, the killing machine of the times.

During the nineteenth century the urge for revolution once again inspired terrorist tactics, this time using newly developed explosives against government officials. A political philosophy known as anarchism arose in Europe and Russia advocating the use of violence to overthrow unjust governments and deliver power to the working classes. Anarchism was responsible for a number of assassinations throughout the century. In Russia, for example, anarchists opposed to the czarist system of government thought that workers would be more likely to be inspired to revolt if they saw evidence that the government was vulnerable to violent attack by assassination or bombing. This strategy, known as "propaganda of the deed," was employed by a small anarchist group in Russia called the Peoples' Will. These anarchists assassinated Czar Alexander II in 1880 using a bomb. Although most of those involved with the assassination were either executed or imprisoned—and another, more repressive czar quickly replaced Alexander II—the terrorist act may have marked the beginning of the end of the czarist system. In 1917 the last czar abdicated the throne, and in October of that year the Bolshevik revolution under Vladimir Lenin began.

The politics and terror tactics of the anarchist movement also invaded America when Russian-born anarchists such as Alexander Berkman and Emma Goldman became involved in the American labor movement. In 1892, for example, these two failed in an attempt to kill Carnegie Steel Company executive William Clay Frick with a bomb in retaliation for the company's shooting of workers during a strike.

Terrorism in the twentieth century continued to be based on political motivations as state terror campaigns developed to repress and control citizenry in Communist and fascist governments. For example, the Bolsheviks in Russia set up an internal security force called the Cheka, which later carried out a policy called the Red Terror aimed at repressing counterrevolutionary threats. Ultimately, the revolution led to the creation of a Communist state and to the rise of Joseph Stalin, who implemented his own well-known campaign of repression and state-run terror. About the same time, in the late 1930s and early 1940s, another dictator, Adolf Hitler of Germany, implemented his own horrific state terror program. Later known as the Holocaust, this program involved the extermination of Jews and other peoples.

The twentieth century also witnessed a multitude of nationalist separatist movements that employed terrorist tactics aimed at replacing governments and fulfilling specific political goals. In the 1920s the Irish rose up against British rule by forming an armed group called the Irish Republican Army (IRA), which began a guerrilla campaign against British military in Ireland. The IRA campaign eventually led to a political solution—a treaty between Britain and Ireland (in 1921) giving predominantly Catholic southern Ireland independence, but retaining Protestant Northern Ireland as part of England. Similarly, during the 1940s Jews who escaped Nazi and European persecution by immigrating to Palestine formed a terrorist group, called the Irgun, to oust the British from that area and create an independent Jewish state. The group quickly succeeded in its efforts, and in 1948 the state of Israel was created. The 1950s awakened an anticolonial revolt in French-controlled Algeria. In 1955 the Front de Liberation Nationale (FLN), a Muslim resistance group, began a campaign of terror that mostly attacked French government targets. It was successful at toppling colonial rule in the 1960s, when France agreed to grant Algeria independence. Also, in Spain at this time, Basque separatists formed the Euskadi ta Askatasuna (ETA), demanding independence in response to repression by the dictator Francisco Franco. Finally, the 1960s saw the beginning of Arab terrorism against what was viewed as the occupying government of Israel. The

Palestine Liberation Organization (PLO) was formed in 1965 to free Palestine from this Israeli occupation, and in 1967 Israel awakened a sleeping dragon by occupying the West Bank area of Palestine. For decades thereafter, the PLO, led by Yasser Arafat, launched bloody terror attacks on Israel. The conflict continues to this day, and many have argued that it can only be solved politically, with an independent state for the Palestinians.

Domestic terrorism by left-wing students, also based on political motives and aimed at government targets, was a predominant theme during the 1960s and 1970s, both in Europe and the United States. In Europe groups such as the Red Brigades in Italy and the Red Army in Germany, espousing opposition to capitalism, imperialism, and colonialism, were successful in several murders and kidnappings of government officials. In the United States the two most prominent groups were the Black Panther Party, which opposed racial discrimination and oppression and took up arms against the police, and the Weather Underground, which primarily bombed government facilities to protest the war in Vietnam. South America experienced similar left-wing terrorist activities. Intensive police targeting of these groups for their criminal activities was generally successful at destroying their terrorist campaigns.

These separatist and student groups saw themselves as freedom fighters for political change or independence. They used the conventional weapons of the age, including machine guns and explosives and, with some exceptions, targeted government officers or buildings, causing relatively limited casualties. These groups believed violence was justified as the only means to acquire independence from governments that oppressed them.

The New Face of Terrorism

During the late twentieth century an important new phenomenon appeared—the worldwide rise of Arab nationalism combined with fundamentalist, radical Islam. Adherents to this strain of Islam condemned its corruption by any non-Muslim influences, especially Western culture, and sought to create Islamic states in the Middle East. The face of terrorism changed as political goals were replaced with religious ones. This radical Islamic trend signaled an erosion of the constraints on the number of casualties in terrorist attacks; September 11, with its thousands of casualties, is the strongest testament of this phenomenon. But even before then, indiscriminate violence was on the rise. Ironically, terrorists who believe they are doing the will of God appear to have fewer concerns about the numbers of innocents killed.

At first Arab nationalism produced secular Arab states, some of which supported the PLO and other terrorist groups worldwide. Libya led the way in 1969, when a group of pro-Arab military officers led by Muammar Qaddafi launched a coup, ending the pro-Western monarchy there and establishing a secular Arab dictatorship. This was the start of a period of state terrorism and state support for terrorist groups during the 1970s and 1980s that made Qaddafi one of the world's most well known terrorists. Another secular Arab country active in supporting terror in recent decades was Iraq. It hosted various small Arab terrorist groups during the 1970s and 1980s and also, in the 1980s, used chemical weapons against its own citizens (a minority group called the Kurds). Iraq's invasion of Kuwait in 1990 and the subsequent military assault, economic sanctions, and weapons inspections by the UN have seriously damaged Saddam Hussein's ability to export or support terror. Instead, Hussein seems dedicated to defending the stability of his regime by building up his own weapons, including weapons of mass destruction.

In 1979 Iran experienced the first fundamentalist Islamic revolution. It was led by Ayatollah Khomeini, who overthrew the pro-Western shah and openly announced his intention to spread the religious revolution throughout the world. Iran soon became, along with Libya and Iraq, one of the world's biggest sponsors of terrorists. Indeed, Iran's encouragement of Iraq's Islamic Shiite population in its opposition to Saddam Hussein's secular rule provoked Iraq to attack Iran in 1980, leading to an eight-year war between the two countries. The Islamic revolution in Iran and its terrorist ideology also touched America as Iranian students seized the American embassy in Tehran in late 1979 to protest the admission of the shah into the United States for medical treatment. Fifty-two American hostages were held for a total of 444 days until their release was negotiated on January 20, 1981. Notably, although Iraq's current regime is a secular dictatorship run by a minority sect of Sunni Arabs, the majority of its population are Islamic Shiite Arabs similar to the Islamic Shiites who started the Islamic revolution in Iran. This Iraqi Shiite population and its history of persecution by the Sunni ruling class leads some to fear the rise of a radical Islamic state in Iraq in the event of a regime change there.

In 1982 Iran sent agents to Lebanon to found a terrorist Islamic group called Hezbollah (or Party of God) dedicated to ousting Israeli forces from that country and fighting Western imperialism. Israeli troops had occupied southern Lebanon to protect Israel's northern border from Palestinian guerrilla attacks. Hezbollah, after terrorist strikes on both Israeli and American soldiers stationed in Beirut, was largely successful in forcing both Israel and the United States to withdraw from Lebanon. The group has since been elected to seats in the Lebanese parliament and advocates the Palestinian cause. Another Islamic terrorist group, Hamas, was formed in 1978 by a different sect of Sunni Muslims to fight for Palestinians. Both Hamas and Hezbollah favor an Islamic state of Palestine rather than the secular Palestinian state sought by Arafat and the PLO, and both groups openly seek the destruction of the state of Israel. These and other similar Arab-Islamic terrorist groups, such as the Popular Front for the Liberation of Palestine and the Palestinian Islamic Jihad, undertake suicide bombings of civilian populations and have played a large role in disrupting the peace process between the PLO and Israel. Particularly in recent years, suicide bombings against Israeli civilians have been on the increase.

Other Islamic extremists have sought to create fundamentalist Islamic revolutions like that in Iran in several other areas. In Egypt, for example, two radical Islamic terrorist groups developed in the 1970s—the Egyptian Islamic Jihad and Jamaat al-Islamiyya—seeking to overthrow that country's secular Arab government. Although unsuccessful in converting Egypt into an Islamic government, Islamic Jihad was responsible for the assassination of Egyptian president Anwar Sadat in 1981. Both groups have ties with al-Qaeda; in fact, the spiritual leader of Jamaat al-Islamiyya (blind cleric Sheikh Omar Abdel Rahman) is jailed in the United States for involvement in the 1993 World Trade Center terrorist attack. In Sudan a militant Islamic group called the National Islamic Front in 1989 overthrew the elected government of Prime Minister Sadiq al-Mahdi in a military coup; since then the country has been a haven for terrorists. Radical Islamic terrorism also arose in 1993 in Algeria. There an Islamic group called the Armed Islamic Group (known by its French acronym GIA) sought to overthrow the secular Algerian government through massacres of civilians, assassinations, and the bombing of foreigners. In addition, the collapse of the Soviet Union in 1991 precipitated a struggle for independence by the Chechens, a fundamentalist Islamic ethnic group that has lived for centuries in the mountainous Caucasus region of Russia. The Chechens have a history of being persecuted by Stalin during World War II. They are supported in their fight by the Islamic world and perhaps also by outside Islamic terrorist groups. Strikes by both the Russian military and the Chechen separatists have killed many civilians, with no end in sight. In October 2002, for example, Chechen rebels seized a theater in Moscow, taking hundreds of civilian hostages and demanding that Russia end its war in Chechnya. The Russian response was to storm the theater with gas weapons, an action that killed the rebels—along with over a hundred hostages.

Lastly but perhaps most significantly, the 1980s and 1990s produced the world's most notorious radical Islamic group—Osama bin Laden's al-Qaeda organization, the group responsible for the September 11, 2001, World Trade Center massacres. Bin Laden, a wealthy Saudi, first used his sizable fortune to recruit and train thousands of Muslim fighters to fight the Soviet Union's invasion of Afghanistan in 1979, with America's blessing. After the Soviets withdrew in 1989, however, bin Laden continued to build his radical Muslim worldwide network and redirected his efforts towards the destruction of the United States and Western influences. Bin Laden's group, unlike many of the other Islamic terrorist groups discussed above, has not aligned itself with any particular movement to create an Islamic state; his goal instead appears to be a generalized anti-Western terror campaign aimed at conducting strikes against civilian American and Western targets around the world with as many casualties as possible. This makes him an infamous cult hero to many disaffected Arabs in the Middle East who resent Western power and success. Also unlike many past terrorist groups, his organization is decentralized, spread around the globe in terrorist cells that appear to exercise a certain amount of autonomy in organizing and executing their activities.

The U.S. war on terror following September 11, 2001, has disrupted al-Qaeda operations, but the group still exists and continues to conduct terrorist strikes on American and Western targets throughout the world. Terrorist strikes at a tourist resort in Bali and a kidnapping in the Philippines in 2002 are believed to be the work of groups with ties to al-Qaeda. And as recently as November 2002, terrorists linked with al-Qaeda struck Israeli targets in Kenya, bombing a hotel, killing ten Kenyans and three Israelis, and attempting to shoot down an Israeli charter plane using modern antiaircraft weaponry. Al-Qaeda is believed to have ties to various radical Islamic groups, such as Hamas, Abu Sayyaf in the Philippines, Jemaah Islamiyah in Indonesia, and various groups in Kashmir.

The Future of the New Terrorism

Experts predict that future terrorism will continue to veer away from its past models—motivated by political or ideological goals and employed with minimum force—toward religious fanaticism similar to what the world is seeing now in al-Qaeda's campaign of terror. These new terrorists seem concerned less with attacking specific government targets or achieving specific goals and more interested in indiscriminate killing of as many civilians as possible, apparently in order to shock the world, expose the weakness of Western, secular powers, and win converts to their particular brand of Islam. Sometimes these terrorists do not even feel the need to seek publicity or claim responsibility for their terrorist attacks, satisfied simply with watching the destruction they cause. In the case of many modern terrorist groups, there is also the element of martyrdom; terrorists are not only willing to kill others, but also willing to sacrifice their own lives in the process. September 11 showed that creative use of conventional weapons such as box cutters can cause large numbers of casualties. The new, troubling trend toward indiscriminate killing becomes much more of a concern, however, if one considers the possibility of the use of weapons of mass destruction. The availability of such weapons has increased in modern times, and since terrorists throughout history have used whatever technology is available at the time—from daggers to bombs to automatic weapons—future terrorists may also use the cutting-edge weaponry of modern times—chemical, biological, and nuclear weapons. This raises the dangerous specter that weapons capable of destroying the planet may be used by terrorist fanatics whose only goal is large-scale death and destruction and who may have no fear of dying themselves. Because nuclear technology is still expensive and hard to acquire, many terrorist groups for now may lack the resources to quickly develop nuclear weaponry. Chemical and biological agents, unfortunately, are relatively inexpensive, easily acquired, and potentially able to cause large-scale suffering (as a sarin gas subway attack in Tokyo revealed in 1995).

However, there are a number of rogue states that either already possess or are developing nuclear capability and other weapons of mass destruction. In addition to the three countries noted by Bush in his "axis of evil" speech (Iraq, Iran, and North Korea), the U.S. government considers Syria, Sudan, and Cuba to be sponsors of terrorism seeking to develop weapons of mass destruction. Considering that these regions may actually contemplate using this nuclear capability against their enemies or perhaps worse, sharing it with international terrorist groups who may have even less hesitation to use it indiscriminately, the civilized world may truly face a new, heretofore unimaginable threat.

GREAT
SPEECHES
IN
HISTORY

Terrorism in History — Revolution, State Terrorism, and Anti-Colonialism

Terror Is Necessary to the French Revolution

Maximilien Robespierre

The French Revolution began late in the eighteenth century as a response to an economic crisis caused, in part, by the extravagances of France's King Louis XVI and his queen, Marie Antoinette. A group of representatives that became known as the National Assembly called for democratic reforms, arrested the king and queen, and later executed them. The National Assembly appointed a twelve-member Committee of Public Safety to run the country. Maximilien Robespierre, a lawyer and accomplished orator, was appointed as a member of the committee.

Largely under Robespierre's direction, the committee quickly took actions to stabilize the French economy and reorganize the army to protect against external threats. Robespierre next turned the committee's attention to eliminating internal threats to the new government, launching a terror campaign known as the "Reign of Terror." The Reign of Terror lasted for only months, but it resulted in more than 250,000 arbitrary arrests and perhaps tens of thousands of deaths. In a speech on February 5, 1794, excerpted below, Robespierre defended the use of terror to protect France's revolution and new government.

The Reign of Terror ended with Robespierre's own death. He believed fellow members of the committee were conspiring against him and sought to have them executed. Instead, they arrested Robespierre, who was shot in the face during the altercation. He spent his last night

---

Maximilien Robespierre, speech to the Committee of Public Safety, February 5, 1794.

TERRORISM

30

in a jail cell with a shattered jaw. The next morning, on
July 28, 1794, Robespierre was guillotined, bringing the
Reign of Terror to an end but leaving France's experiment
with democracy in shambles. France next turned to
Napoleon Bonaparte, who ruled France as a dictator.

To found and consolidate democracy, to achieve the
peaceable reign of the constitutional laws, we must
end the war of liberty against tyranny and pass safely
across the storms of the revolution: such is the aim of the revolutionary system that you have enacted. Your conduct,
then, ought also to be regulated by the stormy circumstances
in which the republic is placed; and the plan of your administration must result from the spirit of the revolutionary government combined with the general principles of democracy.

The Fundamental Principle of Democracy Is Virtue

Now, what is the fundamental principle of the democratic or
popular government—that is, the essential spring which
makes it move? It is virtue; I am speaking of the public virtue
which effected so many prodigies in Greece and Rome and
which ought to produce much more surprising ones in republican France; of that virtue which is nothing other than
the love of country and of its laws. . . .

The whole development of our theory would end here if
you had only to pilot the vessel of the Republic through calm
waters; but the tempest roars, and the revolution imposes on
you another task.

Terror Is Necessary in Times of Revolution

This great purity of the French revolution's basis, the very
sublimity of its objective, is precisely what causes both our
strength and our weakness. Our strength, because it gives to
us truth's ascendancy over imposture, and the rights of the

public interest over private interests; our weakness, because it rallies all vicious men against us, all those who in their hearts contemplated despoiling the people and all those who intend to let it be despoiled with impunity, both those who have rejected freedom as a personal calamity and those who have embraced the revolution as a career and the Republic as prey. Hence the defection of so many ambitious or greedy men who since the point of departure have abandoned us along the way because they did not begin the journey with the same destination in view. The two opposing spirits that have been represented in a struggle to rule nature might be said to be fighting in this great period of human history to fix irrevocably the world's destinies, and France is the scene of this fearful combat. Without, all the tyrants encircle you; within, all tyranny's friends conspire; they will conspire until hope is wrested from crime. We must smother the internal and external enemies of the Republic or perish with it; now in this situation, the first maxim of your policy ought to be to lead the people by reason and the people's enemies by terror.

If the spring of popular government in time of peace is virtue, the springs of popular government in revolution are at once *virtue and terror:* virtue, without which terror is fatal; terror, without which virtue is powerless. Terror is nothing other than justice, prompt, severe, inflexible; it is therefore an emanation of virtue; it is not so much a special principle as it is a consequence of the general principle of democracy applied to our country's most urgent needs.

No Mercy for Enemies of the Revolution

It has been said that terror is the principle of despotic government. Does your government therefore resemble despotism? Yes, as the sword that gleams in the hands of the heroes of liberty resembles that with which the henchmen of tyranny are armed. Let the despot govern by terror his brutalized subjects; he is right, as a despot. Subdue by terror the enemies of liberty, and you will be right, as founders of the Republic. The government of the revolution is liberty's despotism against tyranny. Is force made only to protect crime? And is the thunderbolt not destined to strike the heads of the proud? . . .

Indulgence for the royalists, cry certain men, mercy for the villains! No! mercy for the innocent, mercy for the weak, mercy for the unfortunate, mercy for humanity.

Society owes protection only to peaceable citizens; the only citizens in the Republic are the republicans. For it, the royalists, the conspirators are only strangers or, rather, enemies. This terrible war waged by liberty against tyranny—is it not indivisible? Are the enemies within not the allies of the enemies without? The assassins who tear our country apart, the intriguers who buy the consciences that hold the people's mandate; the traitors who sell them; the mercenary pamphleteers hired to dishonor the people's cause, to kill public virtue, to stir up the fire of civil discord, and to prepare political counterrevolution by moral counterrevolution—are all those men less guilty or less dangerous than the tyrants whom they serve?

Russia Denounces Stalin's Brutal Repression

Nikita Khrushchev

The "October Revolution" of 1917, led by the Bolsheviks under Vladimir Lenin, ended the long history of repressive czarist rule in Russia and replaced it with a Marxist-Leninist socialist government. Under Lenin, Russia set up an internal security force called the Cheka and later developed a policy called the Red Terror aimed at repressing counterrevolutionary threats. After a couple of debilitating strokes in 1922 and 1923, Lenin died in January 1924, leaving Joseph Stalin and Leon Trotsky as the two leading successors. Although Lenin wanted Trotsky to succeed him, Stalin ultimately proved to be stronger, and in 1929 Trotsky was expelled from the Soviet Union, making Stalin the sole leader of the Communist Party and of the Soviet Union. Stalin thereafter became one of the most repressive dictators in the world, as he implemented a state-run campaign of brutal terror between 1928 and 1934 against anyone labeled an "enemy of the people." Stalin is said to be responsible for the deaths of millions in the Soviet Union. After Stalin's death in 1953, Nikita Khrushchev became first secretary of the Communist Party of the Soviet Union. Three years later, at the Twentieth Party Congress in 1956, Khrushchev denounced Stalin and his "cult of personality," which Khrushchev said led to Stalin's repressive terror program.

Nikita Khrushchev, speech before the Twentieth Party Congress of the Communist Party of the Soviet Union, February 25, 1956.

Comrades, in the report of the Central Committee of the party at the 20th Congress, in a number of speeches by delegates to the Congress, as also formerly during the plenary CC/CPSU sessions, quite a lot has been said about the cult of the individual and about its harmful consequences. . . .

Marx and Lenin Denounced the Cult of the Individual

Allow me first of all to remind you how severely the classics of Marxism-Leninism [the communist philosophy developed by Karl Marx and Vladimir Lenin] denounced every manifestation of the cult of the individual. In a letter to the German political worker, Wilhelm Bloss, Marx stated: "From my antipathy to any cult of the individual, I never made public during the existence of the International the numerous addresses from various countries which recognized my merits and which annoyed me. I did not even reply to them, except sometimes to rebuke their authors. Engels and I first joined the secret society of Communists on the condition that everything making for superstitious worship of authority would be deleted from its statute.". . .

The great modesty of the genius of the revolution, Vladimir Ilyich Lenin, is known. Lenin had always stressed the role of the people as the creator of history, the directing and organizational role of the party as a living and creative organism, and also the role of the central committee.

Marxism does not negate the role of the leaders of the workers' class in directing the revolutionary liberation movement.

While ascribing great importance to the role of the leaders and organizers of the masses, Lenin at the same time mercilessly stigmatized every manifestation of the cult of the individual, inexorably combated the foreign-to-Marxism views about a "hero" and a "crowd" and countered all efforts to oppose a "hero" to the masses and to the people.

Lenin taught that the party's strength depends on its indissoluble unity with the masses, on the fact that behind the party follow the people—workers, peasants and intelligentsia. "Only he will win and retain the power," said Lenin, "who believes in the people, who submerges himself in the fountain of the living creativeness of the people.". . .

During Lenin's life the central committee of the party was a real expression of collective leadership of the party and of the Nation. Being a militant Marxist-revolutionist, always unyielding in matters of principle, Lenin never imposed by force his views upon his coworkers. He tried to convince; he patiently explained his opinions to others. Lenin always diligently observed that the norms of party life were realized, that the party statute was enforced, that the party congresses and the plenary sessions of the central committee took place at the proper intervals.

Lenin Warned of Stalin's Abuse of Power

In addition to the great accomplishments of V.I. Lenin for the victory of the working class and of the working peasants, for the victory of our party and for the application of the ideas of scientific communism to life, his acute mind expressed itself also in that he detected in Stalin in time those negative characteristics which resulted later in grave consequences. Fearing the future fate of the party and of the Soviet nation, V.I. Lenin made a completely correct characterization of Stalin, pointing out that it was necessary to consider the question of transferring Stalin from the position of Secretary General because of the fact that Stalin is excessively rude, that he does not have a proper attitude toward his comrades, that he is capricious, and abuses his power. . . .

Vladimir Ilyich said: "Stalin is excessively rude, and this defect, which can be freely tolerated in our midst and in contacts among us Communists, becomes a defect which cannot be tolerated in one holding the position of the Secretary General. Because of this, I propose that the comrades consider the method by which Stalin would be removed from this position and by which another man would be selected for it, a man, who above all, would differ from Stalin in only one quality, namely, greater tolerance, greater loyalty, greater kindness, and more considerate attitude toward the comrades, a less capricious temper, etc."

Stalin's Repression of All "Enemies of the People"

As later events have proven, Lenin's anxiety was justified; in the first period after Lenin's death Stalin still paid attention to his (i.e., Lenin's) advice, but, later be began to disregard the serious admonitions of Vladimir Ilyich.

When we analyze the practice of Stalin in regard to the direction of the party and of the country, when we pause to consider everything which Stalin perpetrated, we must be convinced that Lenin's fears were justified. The negative characteristics of Stalin, which, in Lenin's time, were only incipient, transformed themselves during the last years into a grave abuse of power by Stalin, which caused untold harm to our party. . . .

Stalin acted not through persuasion, explanation, and patient cooperation with people, but by imposing his concepts and demanding absolute submission to his opinion. Whoever opposed this concept or tried to prove his viewpoint, and the correctness of his position, was doomed to removal from the leading collective and to subsequent moral and physical annihilation. This was especially true during the period following the 17th party congress, when many prominent party leaders and rank-and-file party workers, honest and dedicated to the cause of communism, fell victim to Stalin's despotism. . . .

Stalin originated the concept enemy of the people. This term automatically rendered it unnecessary that the ideological errors of a man or men engaged in a controversy be proven; this term made possible the usage of the most cruel repression, violating all norms of revolutionary legality, against anyone who in any way disagreed with Stalin, against those who were only suspected of hostile intent, against those who had bad reputations. This concept, enemy of the people, actually eliminated the possibility of any kind of ideological fight or the making of one's views known on this or that issue, even those of a practical character. In the main, and in actuality, the only proof of guilt used, against all norms of current legal science, was the confession of the accused himself, and, as subsequent probing proved, confessions were ac-

quired through physical pressures against the accused. . . .
Lenin used severe methods only in the most necessary
cases, when the exploiting classes were still in existence and
were vigorously opposing the revolution, when the struggle
for survival was decidedly assuming the sharpest forms, even
including a civil war. Stalin, on the other hand, used extreme
methods and mass repressions at a time when the revolution
was already victorious, when the Soviet state was strengthened, when the exploiting classes were already liquidated,
and Socialist relations were rooted solidly in all phases of national economy, when our party was politically consolidated
and had strengthened itself both numerically and ideologically. It is clear that here Stalin showed in a whole series of
cases his intolerance, his brutality, and his abuse of power.
Instead of proving his political correctness and mobilizing
the masses, he often chose the path of repression and physical annihilation, not only against actual enemies, but also
against individuals who had not committed any crimes
against the party and the Soviet Government. Here we see no
wisdom but only a demonstration of the brutal force which
had once so alarmed V.I. Lenin. . . .

Stalin's Terror After the 17th Party Congress

Considering the question of the cult of an individual we must
first of all show everyone what harm this caused to the interests of our party. . . .

In practice Stalin ignored the norms of party life and
trampled on the Leninist principle of collective party leadership. Stalin's willfulness vis-a-vis the party and its central
committee became fully evident after the 17th party congress, which took place in 1934. . . . It was determined that
of the 139 members and candidates of the party's Central
Committee who were elected at the 17th congress, 98 persons, that is, 70 percent, were arrested and shot (mostly in
1937–38). . . . The same fate met not only the central committee members but also the majority of the delegates to the
17th party congress. Of 1,966 delegates with either voting or
advisory rights, 1,108 persons were arrested on charges of

anti-revolutionary crimes, i.e., decidedly more than a majority. This very fact shows how absurd, wild, and contrary to commonsense were the charges of counter-revolutionary crimes made out, as we now see, against a majority of participants at the 17th party congress. . . .

What is the reason that mass repressions against activists increased more and more after the 17th party congress? It was because at that time Stalin had so elevated himself above the party and above the nation that he ceased to consider either the central committee or the party. While he still reckoned with the opinion of the collective before the 17th congress, after the complete political liquidation of the Trotskyites, Zinovievites and Bukharinites [competing communist factions], when as a result of that fight and Socialist victories the party achieved unity, Stalin ceased to an ever greater degree to consider the members of the party's central committee and even the members of the Political Bureau. Stalin thought that now he could decide all things alone and all he needed were statisticians; he treated all others in such a way that they could only listen to and praise him.

[Thereafter] . . . , mass repressions and brutal acts of violation of Socialist legality began. On the evening of December 1, 1934, on Stalin's initiative (without the approval of the Political Bureau—which was passed 2 days later, casually) the Secretary of the Presidium of the Central Executive Committee, Yenukidze, signed the following directive:

> I. Investigative agencies are directed to speed up the cases of those accused of the preparation or execution of acts of terror.
>
> II. Judicial organs are directed not to hold up the execution of death sentences pertaining to crimes of this category in order to consider the possibility of pardon, because the Presidium of the Central Executive Committee, U.S.S.R, does not consider as possible the receiving of petitions of this sort.
>
> III. The organs of the Commissariat of Internal Affairs are directed to execute the death sentences against criminals of the above-mentioned category immediately after the passage of sentences.

This directive became the basis for mass acts of abuse against Socialist legality. During many of the fabricated court cases the accused were charged with "the preparation" of terroristic acts; this deprived them of any possibility that their cases might be reexamined, even when they stated before the court that their confessions were secured by force, and when, in a convincing manner, they disproved the accusations against them. . . .

Mass repressions grew tremendously from the end of 1936 after a telegram from Stalin and [Communist leader Andrei] Zhdanov, dated from Sochi on September 25, 1936, was addressed to [Lazer] Kaganovich, [Vyacheslav] Molotov, and other members of the Political Bureau. The content of the telegram was as follows: "We deem it absolutely necessary and urgent that Comrade [Nikolai] Yezhov be nominated to the post of People's Commissar for Internal Affairs. [Genrikh] Yagoda has definitely proved himself to be incapable of unmasking the Trotskyite-Zinovievite bloc. The OGPU [Soviet secret police] is 4 years behind in this matter. This is noted by all party workers and by the majority of the representatives of the NKVD [People's Commissariat for Internal Affairs, OGPU's predecessor]." Strictly speaking we should stress that Stalin did not meet with and therefore could not know the opinion of party workers. . . .

Trotskyites Were Not a Threat

The mass repressions at this time were made under the slogan of a fight against the Trotskyites. Did the Trotskyites at this time actually constitute such a danger to our party and to the Soviet state? We should recall that in 1927, on the eve of the 15th party congress, only some 4,000 votes were cast for the Trotskyite-Zinovievite opposition, while there were 724,000 for the party line. During the 10 years which passed between the 15th party congress and the February-March central committee plenum, Trotskyism was completely disarmed; many former Trotskyites had changed their former views and worked in the various sectors building socialism. It is clear that in the situation of Socialist victory there was no basis for mass terror in the country. . . .

Communism Will Overcome the Cult of the Individual

Comrades, the 20th Congress of the Communist Party of the Soviet Union has manifested with a new strength the unshakable unity—of our party, its cohesiveness around the central committee, its resolute will to accomplish the great task of building communism. And the fact that we present in all the ramifications the basic problems of overcoming the cult of the individual which is alien to Marxism-Leninism, as well as the problem of liquidating its burdensome consequences, is an evidence of the great moral and political strength of our party. We are absolutely certain that our party, armed with the historical resolutions of the 20th Congress, will lead the Soviet people along the Leninist path to new successes, to new victories. Long live the victorious banner of our party—Leninism.

Nazi Leaders Are Symbols of Terrorism

Robert H. Jackson

World War II ended in 1945, after Britain, the United States, and Russia invaded Germany. Although Adolf Hitler, leader of the Nazi Party in Germany and architect of the Holocaust, committed suicide at the end of the war, many other leaders of the Nazi Party were arrested. After the war, the Allied powers—Britain, the United States, France, and Russia—decided to punish those responsible for war crimes.

The International Military Tribunal was created to try twenty-four Nazi leaders in Nuremberg, Germany, the site of many Nazi rallies during Hitler's rule. Each of the four countries provided one judge, an alternate judge, and prosecutors, and the trials began on November 21, 1945. On that date, Robert H. Jackson, chief counsel for the United States, gave the opening statement for the United States, excerpted here, calling the Nazi leaders symbols of racial hatred, terrorism, arrogance, and the cruel misuse of power.

The defendants were charged with conspiracy to commit crimes against peace; planning, initiating, and waging wars of aggression; war crimes; and crimes against humanity. Over the next 218 days, the tribunal heard 230 witnesses, and in October 1946, verdicts were announced ranging from prison terms to death sentences for the defendants. The Nuremberg trials greatly influenced the development of a system of international crimi-

Robert H. Jackson, opening address before the Nuremberg International Military Tribunal, November 21, 1945.

nal law and led to a movement for the establishment of a permanent international criminal court—an effort that finally succeeded in July 2002 (despite U.S. opposition).

May it please Your Honors,
The privilege of opening the first trial in history for crimes against the peace of the world imposes a grave responsibility. The wrongs which we seek to condemn and punish have been so calculated, so malignant and so devastating, that civilization cannot tolerate their being ignored because it cannot survive their being repeated. That four great nations, flushed with victory and stung with injury stay the hand of vengeance and voluntarily submit their captive enemies to the judgment of the law is one of the most significant tributes that Power ever has paid to Reason.

This tribunal, while it is novel and experimental, is not the product of abstract speculations nor is it created to vindicate legalistic theories. This inquest represents the practical effort of four of the most mighty of nations, with the support of seventeen more, to utilize International Law to meet the greatest menace of our times—aggressive war. The common sense of mankind demands that law shall not stop with the punishment of petty crimes by little people. It must also reach men who possess themselves of great power and make deliberate and concerted use of it to set in motion evils which leave no home in the world untouched. It is a cause of this magnitude that the United Nations will lay before Your Honors.

Prisoners Are Symbols of Hatred, Terrorism, and Violence

In the prisoners' dock sit twenty-odd broken men. Reproached by the humiliation of those they have led almost as bitterly as by the desolation of those they have attacked, their personal capacity for evil is forever past. It is hard now to perceive in these miserable men as captives the power by which as Nazi leaders they once dominated much of the world and terrified most of it. Merely as individuals, their fate is of little consequence to the world.

What makes this inquest significant is that those prisoners represent sinister influence that will lurk in the world long after their bodies have returned to dust. They are living symbols of racial hatreds, of terrorism and violence, and of the arrogance and cruelty of power. They are symbols of fierce nationalism and militarism, of intrigue and war-making which have embroiled Europe generation after generation, crushing its manhood, destroying its homes, and impoverishing its life. They have so identified themselves with the philosophies they conceived and with the forces they directed that any tenderness to them is a victory and an encouragement to all the evils which are attached to their names. Civilization can afford no compromise with the social forces which would gain renewed strength if we deal ambiguously or indecisively with the men in whom those forces now precariously survive.

The Damage Done

What these men stand for we will patiently and temperately disclose. We will give you undeniable proofs of incredible events. The catalogue of crimes will omit nothing that could be conceived by a pathological pride, cruelty, and lust for power. These men created in Germany, under the *Fuehrerprinzip*, a National Socialist despotism equalled only by the dynasties of the ancient East. They took from the German people all those dignities and freedoms that we hold natural and inalienable rights in every human being. The people were compensated by inflaming and gratifying hatreds toward those who were marked as "scape-goats." Against their opponents, including Jews, Catholics, and free labor the Nazis directed such a campaign of arrogance, brutality, and annihilation as the world has not witnessed since the pre-Christian ages. They excited the German ambition to be a "master race," which of course implies serfdom for others. They led their people on a mad amble for domination. They diverted social energies and resources to the creation of what they thought to be an invincible war machine. They overran their neighbors. To sustain the "master race" in its war making, they enslaved millions of human beings and brought them into Germany, where these hapless creatures now wander as "displaced persons." At length bestiality and bad faith reached such excess that they aroused the sleeping strength of imperiled civilization. Its united efforts have ground the German war machine to fragments. But the struggle has left Europe a liberated yet prostrate land where a demoralized society struggles to survive. These are the fruits of the sinister forces that sit with these defendants in the prisoners' dock. . . .

Justice Must Be Done

Unfortunately, the nature of these crimes is such that both prosecution and judgment must be by victor nations over vanquished foes. The worldwide scope of the aggressions carried out by these men has left but few real neutrals. Either the victors must judge the vanquished or we must leave the defeated to judge themselves. After the First World War, we learned the futility of the latter course. The former high station of these defendants, the notoriety of their acts, and the adaptability of their conduct to provoke retaliation make it hard to distinguish between the demand for a just and measured retribution, and the unthinking cry for vengeance which arises from the anguish of war. It is our task, so far as humanly possible, to draw the line between the two. We must never forget that the record on which we judge these defendants today is the record on which history will judge us tomorrow. To pass these defendants a poisoned chalice is to put it to our own lips as well. We must summon such detachment and intellectual integrity to our task that this trial will commend itself to posterity as fulfilling humanity's aspirations to do justice. . . .

If these men are the first war leaders of a defeated nation to be prosecuted in the name of the law, they are also the first to be given a chance to plead for their lives in the name of the law. Realistically, the Charter of this Tribunal, which gives them a hearing, is also the source of their only hope. It may be that these men of troubled conscience, whose only wish is that the world forget them, do not regard a trial as a favor. But they do have a fair opportunity to defend themselves—a favor which these men, when in power, rarely extended to their fellow countrymen. Despite the fact that public opinion already condemns their acts, we agree that here they must be given a presumption of innocence, and we accept the burden of proving criminal acts and the responsibility of these defendants for their commission.

When I say that we do not ask for convictions unless we prove crime, I do not mean mere technical or incidental transgression of international conventions. We charge guilt on planned and intended conduct that involves moral as well as legal wrong. And we do not mean conduct that is a natural and human, even if illegal, cutting of corners, such as many of us might well have committed had we been in the defendants' positions. It is not because they yielded to the normal frailties of human beings that we accuse them. It is their abnormal and inhuman conduct which brings them to this bar.

Evidence Will Show Guilt

We will not ask you to convict these men on the testimony of their foes. There is no count of the Indictment that cannot be proved by books and records. The Germans were always meticulous record keepers, and these defendants had their share of the Teutonic passion for thoroughness in putting things on paper. Nor were they without vanity. They arranged frequently to be photographed in action. We will show you their own films. You will see their own conduct and hear their own voices as these defendants reenact for you, from the screen, some of the events in the course of the conspiracy.

We would also make clear that we have no purpose to incriminate the whole German people. We know that the Nazi Party was not put in power by a majority of the German vote. We know it came to power by an evil alliance between the most extreme of the Nazi revolutionists, the most unrestrained of the German reactionaries, and the most aggressive of the German militarists. If the German populace had willingly accepted the Nazi program, no Stormtroopers would have been needed in the early days of the Party and there would have been no need for concentration camps or the Gestapo, both of which institutions were inaugurated as

soon as the Nazis gained control of the German state. Only after these lawless innovations proved successful at home were they taken abroad.

The German people should know by now that the people of the United States hold them in no fear, and in no hate. It is true that the Germans have taught us the horrors of modern warfare, but the ruin that lies from the Rhine to the Danube shows that we, like our Allies, have not been dull pupils. If we are not awed by German fortitude and proficiency in war, and if we are not persuaded of their political maturity, we do respect their skill in the arts of peace, their technical competence, and the sober, industrious and self- disciplined character of the masses of the German people. In 1933, we saw the German people recovering prestige in the commercial, industrial and artistic world after the set-back of the last war. We beheld their progress neither with envy nor malice. The Nazi regime interrupted this advance. The recoil of the Nazi aggression has left Germany in ruins. The Nazi readiness to pledge the German word without hesitation and to break it without shame has fastened upon German diplomacy a reputation for duplicity that will handicap it for years. Nazi arrogance has made the boast of the "master race" a taunt that will be thrown at Germans the world over for generations. The Nazi nightmare has given the German name a new and sinister significance throughout the world which will retard Germany a century. The German, no less than the non-German world, has accounts to settle with these defendants.

Germany's Illegal War

The fact of the war and the course of the war, which is the central theme of our case, is history. From September 1, 1939, when the German armies crossed the Polish frontiers, until September, 1942, when they met epic resistance at Stalingrad, German arms seemed invincible. Denmark and Norway, the Netherlands and France, Belgium and Luxembourg, the Balkans and Africa, Poland and the Baltic States, and parts of Russia, all had been overrun and conquered by swift, powerful, well-aimed blows. That attack upon the peace of the world is the crime against international society which brings into international cognizance crimes in its aid and preparation which otherwise might be only internal concerns. It was aggressive war, which the nations of the world had renounced. It was war in violation of treaties, by which the peace of the world was sought to be safeguarded.

This war did not just happen—it was planned and prepared for over a long period of time and with no small skill and cunning. The world has perhaps never seen such a concentration and stimulation of the energies of any people as that which enabled Germany twenty years after it was defeated, disarmed, and dismembered to come so near carrying out its plan to dominate Europe. Whatever else we may say of those who were the authors of this war, they did achieve a stupendous work in organization, and our first task is to examine the means by which these defendants and their fellow conspirators prepared and incited Germany to go to war.

The Leaders of the Nazi Plan

In general, our case will disclose these defendants all uniting at some time with the Nazi Party in a plan which they well knew could be accomplished only by an outbreak of war in

Europe. Their seizure of the German state, their subjugation of the German people, their terrorism and extermination of dissident elements, their planning and waging of war, their calculated and planned ruthlessness in the conduct of warfare, their deliberate and planned criminality toward conquered peoples, all these are ends for which they acted in concert; and all these are phases of the conspiracy, a conspiracy which reached one goal only to set out for another and more ambitious one. We shall also trace for you the intricate web of organizations which these men formed and utilized to accomplish these ends. We will show how the entire structure of offices and officials was dedicated to the criminal purposes and committed to use of the criminal methods planned by these defendants and their co-conspirators, many of whom war and suicide have put beyond reach.

It is my purpose to open the case, particularly under Count One of the Indictment, and to deal with the common plan or conspiracy to achieve ends possible only by resort to crimes against peace, war crimes, and crimes against humanity. My emphasis will not be on individual barbarities and perversions which may have occurred independently of any central plan. One of the dangers ever present is that this trial may be protracted by details of particular wrongs and that we will become lost in a "wilderness of single instances." Nor will I now dwell on the activity of individual defendants except as it may contribute to exposition of the common plan.

The case as presented by the United States will be concerned with the brains and authority back of all the crimes. These defendants were men of a station and rank which does not soil its own hands with blood. They were men who knew how to use lesser folk as tools. We want to reach the planners and designers, the inciters and leaders without whose evil architecture the world would not have been for so long scourged with the violence and lawlessness, and wracked with the agonies and convulsions, of this terrible war.

The Nazi Party

The chief instrumentality of cohesion in plan and action was the National Socialist German Workers Party, known as the

Nazi Party. Some of the defendants were with it from the beginning. Others joined only after success seemed to have validated its lawlessness or power had invested it with immunity from the processes of the law. Adolf Hitler became its supreme leader or fuehrer in 1921.

On the 24th of February, 1920, at Munich, it publicly had proclaimed its program (170-PS). Some of its purposes would commend themselves to many good citizens, such as the demands for "profit-sharing in the great industries," "generous development of provision for old age," "creation and maintenance of a healthy middle class," "a land reform suitable to our national requirements," and "raising the standard of health." It also made a strong appeal to that sort of nationalism which in ourselves we call patriotism and in our rivals chauvinism. It demanded "equality of rights for the German people in its dealing with other nations and the evolution of the peace treaties of Versailles and St. Germaine." It demanded the "union of all Germans on the basis of the right of self-determination of peoples to form a Great Germany." It demanded "land and territory (colonies) for the enrichment of our people and the settlement of our surplus population." All these, of course, were legitimate objectives if they were to be attained without resort to aggressive warfare.

The Nazi Party from its inception, however, contemplated war. It demanded "the abolition of mercenary troops and the formation of a national army." It proclaimed that "In view of the enormous sacrifice of life and property demanded of a nation by every war, personal enrichment through war must be regarded a crime against the nation. We demand, therefore, the ruthless confiscation of all war profits." I do not criticize this policy, indeed, I wish it were universal. I merely point out that in a time of peace, war was a preoccupation of the Party, and it started the work of making war less offensive to the masses of the people. With this it combined a program of physical training and sports for youth that became, as we shall see, the cloak for a secret program of military training.

Israel Was Born from Armed Struggle Against British Colonial Rule

Menachem Begin

Britain took control of the area known as Palestine from the Turkish Ottoman Empire in 1918, at a time when the area was occupied largely by Arabs. The British allowed Jews to immigrate to Palestine to escape persecution in Europe during the 1920s and 1930s. During World War II, the Jews in Palestine demanded their own government in Palestine and instituted a campaign of terrorism against British rule.

The group that led this terrorist effort was the Irgun, headed by Menachem Begin, who later became prime minister of Israel. In the early 1940s, the British adamantly adhered to their policy of not allowing further immigration of Jews to Israel, despite the emerging news of the extent of the Holocaust. In response, beginning in 1943, the Irgun undertook a series of brutal terrorist attacks against the British, including a famous 1946 attack on the King David Hotel, the headquarters of British military and civilian administration in Palestine, which killed ninety-one and injured forty-five. Other attacks by Irgun included the bombing of British immigration offices, intelligence centers, and police stations. Irgun ultimately contributed to ousting the British from Israel, and in 1947, the United Nations voted to partition Palestine and create a separate Jewish state. In the following excerpts

Menachem Begin, "Speech of the Commander-in-Chief of the Irgun Zvai Leumi," *Psychological Warfare and Propaganda*, edited by Eli Tavin and Yonah Alexander. Wilmington, DE: Scholarly Resources Inc., 1982.

from a speech Begin made on May 15, 1948, just after
the state of Israel was created, Begin defended Irgun's
armed struggle against British rule.

Begin later founded the right-wing Herut Party in Israel, which eventually became the Likud Party. In 1977,
he became prime minister of Israel and pursued peace
talks with Arab countries, leading to a 1979 Egypt–Israel
peace treaty, for which Begin and Egyptian president
Anwar Sadat were jointly awarded the Nobel Peace Prize.

Citizens of the Hebrew homeland, soldiers of Israel,
Hebrew youth, Sisters and Brothers in Zion;
After many years of underground warfare, years
of persecution and suffering, moral and physical suffering,
the rebels against the enslaver stand before you with a blessing of thanks on their lips and a prayer in their heart. The
blessing is the one their forefathers used to greet holidays
with. It was with this blessing that they tasted new fruit. And
it is truly a holiday in our dwellings and a new fruit is visible
before our very eyes. The Hebrew revolt of 1944–48 has
been crowned with success, the first Hebrew revolt since the
Hasmonean insurrection [a Jewish revolt in 166 B.C. against
Greek rule], that has ended in victory. The rule of enslavement of Britain in our country has been beaten, uprooted,
has crumbled and been dispersed. The State of Israel has
arisen out of a bloody battle, a battle of conquest. The road
for the mass return to Zion has been paved. The basis has
been laid—but only the basis—for actual Hebrew independence. One phase of the battle for freedom whose aim it was
to return the entire People of Israel to its homeland and return the entire Land of Israel to its nation—its owner, has
ended. But only one phase. And if we keep in mind that this
great event has happened after seventy generations of disper-
sion, of disarmament, of enslavement, of neverending wan-
derings and persecution; if we remember that this thing has
happened in the midst of the total campaign of extermination
of the Jew wherever he be; if we remember that once again
the few overcame the many who would destroy Israel—then,

despite the fact that the cup of suffering of our mothers and children has not yet been emptied, it is our right and our duty to give thanks, most humbly, to the Rock and Saviour of Israel for the miracles he has shown our people this day, even as in days of yore. Therefore we shall say today—the first day of our liberation from the yoke of the British enslaver—Blessed be He who kept us alive and brought us hence.

The Difficult Road to Statehood

The State of Israel has arisen. And it has arisen "Only Thus": Through blood, fire, a strong hand and a mighty arm, with sufferings and sacrifices. It could not be otherwise. . . . And in truth, Brothers in Zion, it was difficult for us to erect our state. Tens of generations of wandering from one land of massacre to another were needed; it was necessary that there be exiles, stakes and torture cells; there were needed horrible awakenings out of illusions; there were needed warnings—unheeded warnings—of prophets and seers; there was needed the labour of generations of pioneers and builders; and there was need of an uprising of rebels, to crush the enemy; there was need of gallows and exiles beyond seas and deserts—all this was necessary in order that we might reach the stage where there are seven hundred thousand [in our] homeland, to the state where the direct rule of oppression has been driven out and independence declared in part of the country, the whole of which is ours.

The Future of Algeria Cannot Be Forced by Terror

Charles de Gaulle

France invaded Algeria in 1830 and made it part of its colonial empire, leading to an upper class of French colonists, or colons, and a native underclass. In 1955, the Front de Liberation Nationale (FLN), a Muslim resistance group, began a campaign of terror aimed at toppling colonial rule. The group waged a guerrilla war against French government targets (such as buildings, military and police posts, and communications installations) and sometimes attacked civilians. Despite French efforts to crush the rebellion, it continued and spawned counterterrorist fighting by the colons. The colons demanded that Charles de Gaulle, who was prominent in the French government before World War II and leader of the French resistance against Germany during the war, be returned to power to deal with the Algerian conflict.

In 1958, Charles de Gaulle was appointed prime minister of France (he was later elected president of France). Although expected to support the colons, he instead in the following 1959 speech declared that Algerians had the right to self-determination. In the same speech, de Gaulle cautioned the insurgents that France would enforce the freedom of choice for Algerians and not allow the future of Algeria to be determined by force or terror. In 1961, despite violent opposition by the European colons, France began negotiations with the FLN, leading to a peace agreement signed in 1962 and a refer-

Charles de Gaulle, radio and television broadcast, September 16, 1959.

endum that same year in which the majority of Algerians voted for independence.

After Algeria gained its independence, the colonial European settlers evacuated in droves, leaving the country with a lack of skilled labor and a struggling economy. Ahmed Ben Bella, leader of the FLN, was elected the first president of Algeria but was unable to solve the country's economic problems during his term. In 1965, Defense Minister Houari Boumedienne led a bloodless coup that overthrew Ben Bella and the FLN and instituted a one-party socialist government in the country. After Boumedienne's death, his successor was forced to institute reforms allowing for multiple party elections due to a rising tide of Islamic fundamentalist protests. In 1990, an Islamic group advocating an Islamic state—called the Islamic Salvation Front (FIS)—won an overwhelming victory. The government opposed the FIS and disbanded elections, leading to an FIS terror campaign and war between government forces and militants that continues to the present day.

F rance is still faced with a difficult and bloody problem: that of Algeria. This we must solve. We will certainly not do so by tossing at each other empty and oversimplified slogans, on one side or the other, both of which are blind to everything save their conflicting passions, interests or daydreams. We will solve it as a great nation should do, choosing the only path worthy of being followed. I mean the free choice which the Algerians themselves will make for their future.

The First Step—Pacification

As a matter of fact, much has already been done to pave the way for this solution. Through pacification first of all, for nothing can be solved against a background of shooting and assassination. From that point of view, I do not claim that we have reached the end of the road. But I say that there is no comparison, in terms of the safety of persons and property, between the situation which prevailed two or three years ago and that which prevails now. Our Army is accomplishing its mission both courageously and skillfully, fighting its opponents while maintaining with the population deeper and broader contacts than had ever existed before. If our soldiers, and in particular, the 120,000 Moslems among them, had faltered in their duty or if the Algerian masses had turned against France, that indeed would have spelled disaster. But since this has not occurred, the restoration of public order, although it may not be imminent, is now in sight.

The Second Step—Universal Suffrage

The second requisite for a settlement is that all Algerians should have the means of expressing themselves through truly universal suffrage. Up to last year they have never had it. They have it now, thanks to the institution of equal rights, a single college, and the fact that the larger communities, those of the Moslems, are sure of obtaining at the polls the largest numbers of representatives elected. This was a change of the greatest significance, actually a revolution. On September 28 of last year, the Algerians, by referendum, adopted the Constitution and signified their intention that their future should be shaped along with France.

On November 30, they elected their Deputies, on April 19, their Municipal Councils, and on May 31, their Senators. No doubt there are some people who claim that, in the situation in which the voters found themselves, under pressure from the forces of law and order and the threats of the insurgents, these elections could be sincere only to a limited extent. They were held, however, in towns and rural areas, and with a large mass of voters; and even at the time of the referendum, participation was widespread, spontaneous and enthusiastic.

At all events the path is open. As soon as violence has subsided, the path may be used even more broadly, and more freely. Next year, the General Councils will be elected, from which, later, will be drawn a number of Administrative, Economic and Social Councils, which will discuss with the Delegate General the development of Algeria.

The Final Step—Social and Economic Development

To solve the problem of Algeria is not merely to restore order or to grant people the right of self-determination. It is also, indeed it is primarily, to deal with a human problem. In Algeria there are populations, whose numbers double every 35 years, on a land that is to a great extent untilled, devoid of mines, of factories or important sources of power; populations, three quarters of which are sunk in a poverty which seems to belong to their very nature. The problem is to give the Algerians the means of supporting themselves by their own work; to see to it that their elites should emerge and be trained, that their soil and subsoil should yield far more and much better products. This implies a vast effort of social and economic development—an effort, indeed, which is already under way.

During the year 1959, France will have spent in Algeria—to mention only public investments and the costs of civil administration—some $400 million. Expenses will rise during the course of the coming years, with the continued implementation of the Constantine Plan [a five-year plan announced by de Gaulle in Constantine, Algeria, to improve conditions for Muslims in Algeria]. Over the past ten months, a hundred industrial concerns have applied for authorization to construct plants. Twenty thousand acres of fertile soil are being allocated to Moslem farmers. There are 50,000 more Algerians working in Metropolitan France. The number of Moslems in public employment has increased by 5,000. At the beginning of the coming school year, schools in Algeria will be enrolling some 860,000 children as against 700,000 at the corresponding time last year and 560,000 the year before. In six weeks the oil at Hassi-Messaoud will be arriving at the coastline at Bougie. In a year, the oil from Edjeleh will be reaching the Gulf of Gabès. In 1960, the gas from Hassi-R'Mel will begin to be distributed in Algiers and Oran, later at Bône. If France is willing, and in a position to continue with the Algerians the task she has undertaken, and of which she alone is capable, then in fifteen years Algeria will be a prosperous and productive land.

France Proclaims Algerians Have a Right to Self-Determination

Thanks to the progress of pacification, to democracy, and to social advancement, we can now look forward to the day when the men and women who live in Algeria will be in a position to decide their own destiny, once and for all, freely and in the full knowledge of what is at stake. Taking into account all these factors—those of the Algerian situation, those inherent in the national and the international situation—I deem it necessary that recourse to self-determination be here and now proclaimed. In the name of France and of the Republic, by virtue of the power granted to me by the Constitution to consult its citizens—if only God lets me live and the people listen to me—I pledge myself to ask the Algerians, on the one hand, in their twelve Departments, what, when all is said and done, they wish to be; and, on the other hand, all Frenchmen, to endorse that choice.

The question, obviously, will be put to the Algerians as individuals. For since the beginning of the world there has never been any Algerian unity, far less any Algerian sovereignty. The Carthaginians, the Romans, the Vandals, the Byzantines, the Syrian Arabs, the Cordova Arabs, the Turks, the French have, one after the other, penetrated the country without there being—at any time, under any shape or form—an Algerian State. As for the time of the elections, I will decide upon it in due course, at the latest four years after the actual restoration of peace; that is to say, once a situation has been established whereby not more than 200 persons a year will lose their lives, either in ambushes or isolated attacks. The ensuing period of time will be devoted to resuming normal existence, to emptying the camps and prisons, to permitting the return of exiles, to restoring the free play of individual and public liberties and to enabling the population to become fully aware of what is at stake. I would like to invite, here and now, observers from all over the world to attend, without hindrance, the final culmination of this process.

But what will this political destiny finally be, for the men and women of Algeria who will choose it, once peace is restored? Everyone knows that in theory it is possible to imagine three solutions. Since it is in the interest of all concerned—and especially of France—that the question be answered without ambiguity, the three conceivable solutions will be put to the vote:

• Either secession, where some believe independence would be found. France would then leave the Algerians who had expressed their wish to become separated from her. They would organize, without her, the territory in which they live, the resources which they have at their disposal, the government which they desire. I am convinced personally that such an outcome would be incredible and disasterous. Algeria being what it is at the present time, and the world what we know it to be, secession would carry in its wake the most appalling poverty, frightful political chaos, widespread slaughter and, soon after, the warlike dictatorship of the Communists. But this demon must be exorcised, and this must be done by the Algerians themselves. If it should appear through some inconceivable misfortune that such is indeed their will, France would undoubtedly stop devoting so many assets and so many billions of francs to a cause shorn of any hope. It goes without saying that, on this assumption, those Algerians, regardless of origin, who might wish to remain French would do so in any case and that France would arrange, if need be, for their regrouping and resettlement. On the other hand, everything would be arranged so that the operation of oil wells, the handling and shipping of Saharan oil—which is the result of French efforts and which is of interest to the whole Western world—would be ensured in any event.

• Or out-and-out identification with France, as is implied in equality of rights: Algerians can accede to all political, administrative and judicial functions of the state and have free access to the public service. They would benefit, as regards salaries, wages, social security, education and vocational training, from all measures provided for in Metropolitan France; they would live and work wherever they saw fit, throughout the territory of the Republic; in other words, they would be living, from every point of view, regardless of their religion or the community to which they belonged, by and large on the same footing and at the same level as other citizens and become part and parcel of the French people who

would then, in effect, spread from Dunkirk to Tamanrasset.
• Or the government of Algerians by Algerians, backed up by French help and in close relationship with her, as regards the economy, education, defense and foreign relations. In that case, the internal regime of Algeria should be of the federal type, so that the various communities—French, Arab, Kabyle, Mozabite—who live together in the country would find guarantees for their own way of life and a framework for cooperation.

The Future of Algerians Cannot Be Forced

But since for a year now it has been settled that—through the institution of equal voting rights, the single college and the emergence of a majority of Moslem representatives—the political future of Algerians is to depend on Algerians; since it has been officially and solemnly emphasized that, once peace has been restored, the Algerians will let it be known what fate they want for themselves, to the exclusion of any other, and that all of them, whatever their program may be, whatever they might have done, wherever they come from, will take part, if they wish to do so, in this vote: what then could be the meaning of rebellion?

If those who lead it claim for all Algerians the right to self-determination, all paths are wide open. If the insurgents fear that in stopping the combat, they will be turned over to justice, then it is entirely up to them to settle with the authorities the conditions for their unhindered return, as I suggested when I offered the peace of the brave. If the men who represent the political organization of the insurrection intend not to be excluded from the debate, or later from the polls, or finally from the institutions which will determine the fate of Algeria and ensure its political life, I proclaim that they will have the same place as all the others—no more, no less— a hearing, a share, a place which will be granted them by the votes of the citizens. Why, then, should the odious strife and the fratricidal murders, which are still drenching the Algerian soil with blood, continue?

Unless it is the work of a group of ambitious agitators,

determined to establish by brute force and terror their totalitarian dictatorship and believing that they will one day obtain from the Republic the privilege of discussing with it the
fate of Algeria, thus building up these agitators into an Algerian government. There is not a chance that France would
lend herself to anything so arbitrary. The future of Algerians
rests with Algerians, not as forced on them by knife and machine gun, but according to the will which they will legiti-
mately express through universal suffrage. With them and
for them, France will see to the freedom of their choice. During the few years which will pass before the deadline we have
set, there will be much to do so that Algeria, when pacified,
can weigh all the factors and consequences of its own decision. I intend to concern myself personally with the task. Furthermore, the procedures of the future vote must in due
course be elaborated and specified. But the road is open. The
decision is taken, the stakes are worthy of France.

GREAT
SPEECHES
IN
HISTORY

Modern International Terrorism — Freedom Fighters or Terrorists?

The Irish Guerrilla War Against British Terror

Michael Collins

British rule in Ireland began in the sixteenth century, when the British gave Irish lands to Protestant settlers from Scotland for the purpose of gaining authority over the predominantly Roman Catholic island. Although there were several earlier revolts against British rule, in the early 1900s various groups were formed dedicated to ousting the British from Ireland, including Sinn Fein, the Irish Republican Brotherhood (IRB), and the Volunteers. The first military strike by the Irish against the British was made by the Volunteers on Easter 1916 in Dublin; the revolt was quickly quelled by the British, but Britain proceeded to execute the Irish rebels, who became instant martyrs for an energized Irish cause.

Thereafter, Sinn Fein grew, subsumed the IRB and the Volunteers, and in 1918 won many seats in Britain's Parliament. Sinn Fein, however, refused to become part of Britain's Parliament and instead set up a separate Irish parliament, called Dail Eireann, with Eamon De Valera as president. Britain refused to recognize the Irish government and an Irish-Anglo war began. Sinn Fein's military wing, the Irish Republican Army (IRA), was commanded by Michael Collins, an Irish patriot who had been an early member of the IRB and had participated in the Easter uprising. Collins set up an intelligence network, smuggled arms, and organized a series of assassinations of British officers. In one of the most famous British-Irish

Michael Collins, speech to the Irish people, 1921.

confrontations, on November 21, 1920, after Collins orchestrated the killing of fourteen British intelligence agents, British troops retaliated by firing machine guns into a civilian crowd watching a football match, killing twelve. This event came to be known as Bloody Sunday. By 1921, the violence had demoralized the British, a truce was declared, and treaty talks began between the two sides. In the following speech given in 1921, after Britain agreed to talks, Collins described the history of the Anglo-Irish war and defended the IRA violence as a necessary response to British "terror."

Collins became one of the IRA's chief negotiators in the talks with Britain, but he was unable to secure a treaty that achieved the ultimate goal of a completely united and independent Ireland. Instead, Collins signed a compromised Anglo-Irish Treaty providing for a new Irish Free State comprised of the southern, predominantly Catholic 26 (out of 32) counties, but keeping Northern Protestant Ireland as part of the British Commonwealth. Collins meant this to be a first step toward eventual unification and full independence, but instead the treaty plunged Ireland into a bloody civil war between those who followed Collins and the anti-treaty forces, known as the Irregulars.

Knowing there would be resistance to the compromise treaty, Collins commented at the time that he may have signed his own death warrant. His words were prophetic: Shortly after the signing of the treaty and after the civil war had begun, on August 22, 1922, Michael Collins was ambushed by an unknown assassin while in his home county visiting troops; he died at the age of thirty-two. Collins is remembered, however, as a beloved Irish patriot.

Following Collins's death, the factionalism in Ireland continued for many decades, with the anti-treaty IRA, and its political wing Sinn Fein, continuing to refuse to recognize the Irish government created by the treaty or the loyalty oath to Britain the treaty required. In the 1970s, a splinter Provisional IRA, or Provos, formed and began a strategy of bombings and shootings that lasted into the

1980s. Eventually, Britain pursued peace negotiations, leading to a 1985 Anglo-Irish Treaty that paved the way for a power-sharing government in Northern Ireland between those seeking a united Ireland and those seeking to remain a part of England. In 1997, Britain negotiated a cease-fire, and in 1998, an agreement provided for power sharing and "decommissioning" of arms, sparking hope that the terrorism in Ireland might come to an end. In 2002, however, these gains were jeopardized when evidence emerged of continuing IRA and Sinn Fein military activity.

We have seen how in ancient Ireland the people were themselves the guardians of their land, doing all for themselves according to their own laws and customs, as interpreted by the Brehons, which gave them security, prosperity, and national greatness, and how this was upset by the English determination to blot out Irish ways, when came poverty, demoralisation and a false respect for English standards and habits.

The English power to do this rested on military occupation and on economic control. It had the added advantage of social influence operating upon a people weakened and demoralised by the state of dependence into which the English occupation had brought them.

Military resistance was attempted. Parliamentary strategy was tried. The attempts did not succeed. They failed because they did not go to the root of the question.

The Irish Rise Up

The real cure had to be started—that the people should recover belief in their own ways and ideas and put them into practice. Secret societies were formed and organised. The Land League came into existence. The Gaelic League came. Sinn Féin grew and developed. All these societies did much. But the effort had to be broadened into a national movement to become irresistible. It became irresistible in the Republican movement when it was backed by sufficient military force to prevent the

English forces from suppressing the national revival. The challenge of Easter Week and its sacrifices increased the growing national self-belief. All these things made a resistance against which the English, with their superior forces, pitted themselves in vain.

Ireland's story from 1918 to 1921 may be summed up as the story of a struggle between our determination to govern ourselves and to get rid of British government and the British determination to prevent us from doing either. It was a struggle between two rival Governments, the one an Irish Government resting on the will of the people and the other an alien Government depending for its existence upon military force—the one gathering more and more authority, the other steadily losing ground and growing ever more desperate and unscrupulous.

All the history of the three years must be read in the light of that fact.

An Irish Government

Ireland had never acquiesced in government by England. Gone for ever were policies which were a tacit admission that a foreign Government could bestow freedom, or a measure of freedom, upon a nation which had never surrendered its national claim.

We could take our freedom. We would set up a Government of our own and defend it. We would take the government out of the hands of the foreigner, who had no right to it, and who could exercise it only by force.

A war was being waged by England and her Allies in defence, it was said, of the freedom of small nationalities, to establish in such nations 'the reign of law based upon the consent of the governed'. We, too, proposed to establish in Ireland 'the reign of law based upon the consent of the governed'.

At the General Election of 1918 the Irish Parliamentary Party was repudiated by the Irish people by a majority of over 70 per cent. And they gave authority to their representatives to establish a National Government. The National Government was set up in face of great difficulties. Dáil Éireann came into being. British law was gradually superseded. Sinn Féin

Courts were set up. Commissions were appointed to investigate and report upon the national resources of the country with a view to industrial revival. Land courts were established which settled long-standing disputes. Volunteer police were enrolled. (They were real police, to protect life and property, not military police and police spies to act with an enemy in attacks upon both.) A loan of £400,000 was raised. The local governing bodies of the country were directed, inspected, and controlled by Dáil Éireann. We established a bank to finance societies which wished to acquire land.

But these facts must be concealed.

The Violent British Response

At first the British were content to ridicule the new Government. Then, growing alarmed at its increasing authority, attempts were made to check its activities by wholesale political arrests.

The final phase of the struggle had begun.

In the first two years all violence was the work of the British armed forces who in their efforts at suppression murdered fifteen Irishmen and wounded nearly 400 men, women, and children. Meetings were broken up everywhere. National newspapers were suppressed. Over 1,000 men and women were arrested for political offences, usually of the most trivial nature. Seventy-seven of the national leaders were deported.

No police were killed during these two years. The only disorder and bloodshed were the work of the British forces.

These forces were kept here or sent here by the British Government to harass the development of Irish self-government. They were intended to break up the national organisation. They were intended to goad the people into armed resistance. Then they would have the excuse which they hoped for. Then they could use wholesale violence, and end up by the suppression of the national movement.

But they did not succeed.

In the municipal elections in January, 1920, the people answered afresh. In the rural elections in May and June, 1920, the people repeated their answer. The people supported their leaders and their policy by even larger majorities than the majorities given by the election in November, 1918. The British Government now decided that a greater effort was needed. The moment had come for a final desperate campaign.

The leading London newspaper, *The Times*, declared in a leading article of November 1st, 1920, that it was 'now generally admitted' that a deliberate policy of violence had been 'conceived and sanctioned in advance by an influential section of the Cabinet'. But to admit such a policy was impossible. It was necessary to conceal the real object of the Reign of Terror, for the destruction of the national movement, which was about to begin.

First, the ground had to be prepared. In August, 1920, a law was passed 'to restore law and order in Ireland'. This law in reality abolished all law in Ireland, and left the lives and property of the people defenceless before the British forces. It facilitated and protected—and was designed to facilitate and protect—those forces in the task they were about to undertake. Coroners' inquests were prohibited, so that no inquiry could be made into the acts of violence contemplated. National newspapers, that could not be trusted to conceal the facts and to publish only supplied information, were suppressed. Newspaper correspondents were threatened.

The ground prepared, special instruments had to be selected. 'It is', said the *London Times,* 'common knowledge that the Black and Tans [a special police force recruited by Britain to fight Irish rebels] were recruited from ex-soldiers for a rough and dangerous task'. This 'rough and dangerous task', which had been 'conceived and sanctioned' by the British Cabinet, was to be carried out under three headings. Certain leading men, and Irish Army officers, were to be murdered, their names being entered on a list 'for definite clearance'. All who worked for or supported the national movement were to be imprisoned, and the general population was to be terrorised into submission. A special newspaper, *The Weekly Summary*, was circulated amongst the Crownage to encourage them in their 'rough and dangerous task'. As an indication of its intention it invited them in an early number 'to make an appropriate hell' in Ireland.

Excuses, for the purpose of concealment, had to be invented. The public had to be prepared for the coming campaign. [British prime minister] Mr. Lloyd George in a speech in Carnarvon, October 7, 1920, spoke of the Irish Republican Army as 'a real murder gang'. We began to hear of 'steps necessary to put down a murderous conspiracy'. 'We have got murder by the throat', said Mr. Lloyd George.

Irish Self-Defence

The murders were the legitimate acts of self-defence which had been forced upon the Irish people by English aggression. After two years of forbearance, we had begun to defend ourselves and the life of our nation. We did not initiate the war, nor were we allowed to select the battleground. When the British Government, as far as lay in its power, deprived the Irish people of arms, and employed every means to prevent them securing arms, and made it a criminal (in large areas a capital) offence to carry arms, and, at the same time, began and carried out a brutal and murderous campaign against them and against their National Government, they deprived themselves of any excuse for their violence and of any cause of complaint against the Irish people for the means they took for their protection.

For all the acts of violence committed in Ireland from 1916 to 1921 England, and England alone, is responsible. She willed the conflict and fixed the form it was to take. On the Irish side it took the form of disarming the attackers. We took their arms and attacked their strongholds. We organised our army and met the armed patrols and military expeditions which were sent against us in the only possible way. We met them by an organised and bold guerilla warfare.

But this was not enough. If we were to stand up against the powerful military organisation arrayed against us something more was necessary than a guerilla war in which small bands of our warriors, aided by their knowledge of the country, attacked the larger forces of the enemy and reduced their numbers. England could always reinforce her army. She could replace every soldier that she lost.

Republic of Ireland and the United Kingdom

But there were others indispensable for her purposes which were not so easily replaced. To paralyse the British machine it was necessary to strike at individuals. Without her spies England was helpless. It was only by means of their accumulated and accumulating knowledge that the British machine could operate.

Without their police throughout the country, how could they find the men they wanted? Without their criminal agents in the capital, how could they carry out that removal of the leaders that they considered essential for their victory? Spies are not so ready to step into the shoes of their departed confederates as are soldiers to fill up the front line in honourable battle. And even when the new spy stepped into the shoes of the old one, he could not step into the old one's knowledge.

The most potent of these spies were Irishmen enlisted in the British service and drawn from the small farmer and labourer class. Well might every Irishman at present ask himself if we were doing a wrong thing in getting rid of the system which was responsible for bringing these men into the ranks of the opponents of their own race.

We struck at individuals, and by so doing we cut their lines of communication and we shook their morale. And we conducted the conflict, difficult as it was, with the unequal terms imposed by the enemy, as far as possible, according to the rules of war. Only the British Government were attacked. Prisoners of war were treated honourably and considerately, and were released after they had been disarmed.

British Terror

On the English side they waged a sort of war, but did not respect the laws and usages of war. When our soldiers fell into their hands they were murderers, to be dealt with by the bullet or the rope of the hangman. They were dealt with mostly by the bullet. Strangely enough, when it became law that prisoners attempting to escape should be shot, a considerable larger number of our prisoners attempted to escape than when the greatest penalty to be expected was recapture.

The fact was that when the men whose names were upon the list were identified at once, they were shot at once. When they were identified during a raid, they were taken away and shot while attempting to escape. Or they were brought to Dublin Castle or other place of detention and questioned under torture, and on refusing to give information were murdered because they revolted, seized arms, and attacked their guards.

For these murders no members of the British forces were brought to justice. The perpetrators were but enforcing the law—restoring law and order in Ireland. . . .

No matter how damaging the evidence, the prisoners were invariably acquitted. Necessarily so. They were but carrying out the duties which they had been specially hired at a very high rate of pay to execute.

To excuse the terrible campaign, the world began to hear of reprisals, the natural outbreaks of the rank and file. A campaign which could no longer be concealed had to be excused—a campaign in which sons were murdered before the eyes of their mothers—in which fathers were threatened with death and done to death because they would not tell the whereabouts of their sons—in which men were made to crawl along the streets, and were taken and stripped and flogged, and sent back naked to their homes—in which towns and villages and homes were burned, and women and children left shivering in the fields.

Excuses were necessary for such deeds, and we began to hear of some hitting back by the gallant men who are doing their duty in Ireland. The London *Westminster Gazette* of October 27, 1920, published a message from their own correspondent at Cork which gives an instance of the way in which these gallant men performed their duty: 'A motor lorry of uniformed men, with blackened faces, arrived in Lixane from the Ballybunion district. Before entering the village they pulled up at the house of a farmer named Patrick McElligott. His two sons were pulled outside the door in night attire in a downpour of rain, cruelly beaten with the butt ends of rifles and kicked. The party then proceeded to the house of a young man named Stephen Grady, where they broke in the door. Grady escaped in his night attire through the back window. Searchlights were turned on him, but he made good his escape through the fields. His assistant, named Nolan, was knocked unconscious on the floor with a rifle, and subsequently brought outside the door almost nude and a tub of water poured over him. The party then broke into the room where Miss Grady and her mother were sleeping, pulled Miss Grady out on the road and cut her hair'.

The account tells of the burning of the creamery and of further escapades of the gallant men on their return through the village.

An instance symbolic of the fight, of the devotion and self-sacrifice on the one side, and the brutish insensibility on the other, was the murder on October 25, 1920, of young Willie Gleeson, of Finaghy, Co. Tipperary. Officers of the British Army Intelligence Staff raided the house of his father, looking for another of his sons. Hearing his father threatened with death if he would not (or could not) disclose where his son was, Willie came from his bed and offered himself in place of his father. The offer was accepted, and he was taken out into the yard and shot dead.

On the same night the same party (presumably) murdered Michael Ryan, of Curraghduff, Co. Tipperary, in the presence of his sister. Ryan was lying ill in bed with pneumonia and the sister described the scene in which one officer held a candle over the bed to give better light to his comrade in carrying out the deed.

Such reprisals could not be explained as a severe hitting back, and a new excuse was forthcoming. They were suggested as a just retribution falling upon murderers.

Mr. Lloyd George was 'firmly convinced that the men who are suffering in Ireland are the men who are engaged in a murderous conspiracy'. At the London Guildhall he announced that the police were 'getting the right men'. As it became more and more difficult to conceal the truth the plea of unpremeditation was dropped, and the violence was explained as legitimate acts of self-defence.

But when the Terror, growing evermore violent, and, consequently, ever more ineffective, failed to break the spirit of the Irish people—failed as it was bound to fail—concealment was no longer possible, and the true explanation was blurted out when Mr. Lloyd George and Mr. Bonar Law declared that their acts were necessary to destroy the authority of the Irish National Government which 'has all the symbols and all the realities of government'.

Invitation to Peace Talks

When such a moment had been reached, there was only one course left open for the British Prime Minister—to invite the Irish leaders, the murderers, and heads of the murder gang to discuss with him terms of peace. The invitation was:

> To discuss terms of peace—to ascertain how the association of Ireland with the community of nations known as the British Empire may best be reconciled with Irish national aspirations.

> We all accepted that invitation.

The Threat of Terrorism Undermines Peace in Ireland

Tony Blair

Peace talks in 1921 between Irish rebels and Britain resulted in an Anglo-Irish Treaty, which awarded most of southern, Catholic Ireland full independence but preserved northern, mostly Protestant Ireland as a part of Britain. Thereafter, the Irish Republican Army (IRA) and its mostly Catholic supporters (called "republicans") continued to fight for a united Ireland that would include Northern Ireland. They were opposed by Northern Ireland Protestants who wanted to retain ties with England (called "unionists"). The conflict continued for many decades.

Finally, Britain began peace negotiations with the Irish Republic government, resulting in the Anglo-Irish agreement of 1985. The agreement encouraged the Irish government to make proposals about Northern Ireland, recognized the objective of a united Ireland (if a majority of voters approved), and led the way to the establishment of a power-sharing government in Northern Ireland in which the two warring sides would both elect representatives to the Northern Irish government. In 1997, a cease-fire was negotiated, and in 1998, the parties agreed to establish the power-sharing government, sparking hope that the terrorism in Ireland might come to an end.

In October 2002, however, the peace process in Northern Ireland suffered a setback after police raids on

Tony Blair, speech on the peace process, Belfast, Northern Ireland, October 17, 2002.

the homes of Sinn Fein officials and the group's offices produced evidence that the IRA was conducting espionage on police, army, and unionist leaders. In response, Protestant unionist politicians threatened to resign, claiming that the IRA was continuing its military activity while its political wing, Sinn Fein, was participating in the government. Tony Blair, Britain's prime minister, in the following speech in Belfast, Northern Ireland, on October 17, 2002, praised the progress toward peace since 1998, and called on the IRA to abandon its paramilitary activity in the interests of peace. The IRA, however, refused to disarm, and Britain has since suspended the power-sharing Assembly.

On the 16th May 1997 that I came to Belfast on my first official visit outside London as prime minister and made a speech here. I said then that it was no accident that I had chosen Northern Ireland for my first visit. I had come because I wanted to explain why I was committed to Northern Ireland and to the people here. I am told I have visited Northern Ireland more than any prime minister before me in five years of office. I have given this part of the UK [United Kingdom] as much energy and commitment as any other, because I value it as part of the UK which it will remain so long as a majority of people here wish to be part of it.

The 1998 Peace Agreement

It is now four-and-a-half years since the Belfast agreement. Let us re-cap for a moment on the scale of what we agreed to do in April 1998. After 30 years of troubles, thousands of deaths, Northern Ireland part of the UK but governed unlike any other part of the UK, its communities divided, its daily life scarred in innumerable ways by sectarian bitterness; after all this, we agreed to shape a new future. Enemies would become not just partners in progress but sit together in government. People who used to advocate the murder of British ministers and security services, would be working with them.

The police, the criminal justice system, the entire apparatus of government would be reformed beyond recognition. People would put all the intransigence and hatred of the past behind them and co-operate. Britain and Ireland would reach a new relationship. The north and south of the island of Ireland would have a new set of institutions to mark change and cooperation within a wider framework of relationships within these islands. Paramilitaries who used to murder each other as a matter of routine would talk to each other and learn to live with each other. One of the most abnormal parts of the continent of Europe, never mind the UK, would become normal.

Did anyone seriously believe it would be easy? Did we seriously entertain the notion that the agreement would be signed on the 10th April 1998 and on the 11th it would all be different?

It was a brave undertaking and a vast one. Even now I think that only in the first flush of a new government could we have contemplated it.

The Struggle of Compromise

And almost immediately the problems began. Prisoner release was there in black and white in the agreement. But who could not understand the anguish of the families of the victims of terrorism when they saw their dearest ones' murderers given a rapturous welcome as they were released? Or those who were prepared to die in the cause of a united Ireland who saw their representatives take their place in a partitionist assembly?

Or as the changes bit in the policing of Northern Ireland, as the RUC [Royal Ulster Constabulary] gave way to the PSNI [Police Service of Northern Ireland], who could not sympathise with the feelings of the former officers and their widows who felt they were stigmatised when all they did was to stand up for law and order against the perpetrators of organised violence? Or as the dissident republicans started their campaign to disrupt the process by a return to the bomb and bullet, who could not imagine the anger of those republicans working for peace, when the security measures of the British government appeared to bear down on them, who supported the process, not on those who detested it?

All the time, of course, the malignant whisperings of those opposed to the process, always pointing out its faults, never aiding its strengths; and the evil violence from dissidents, from so-called loyalists, designed to re-ignite sectarian hatred to convulse such progress as we have made. At every step, those working for peace, trying to make the agreement function, were being undermined, often from within their own community. . . .

I watched it all, participated in the crises, made what I could of what I had before me. It has been four and a half years of hassle, frustration and messy compromise. After the dawn of the agreement itself, there have been no moments of dazzling light when the decisions are plain, the good and the bad illuminated with crystal certainty, the path clear, the clarion call easy to sound. Each step has been a struggle. Each bit of advance ground out. . . .

The Progress Made

But let me state this with passion. I have not regretted for one second the effort or the hassle or the compromise. Because along with all of that, anyone can see there has also been progress.

Yes, there is still violence, but at a far, far reduced rate— in 1972, 470 people died. This year, so far, 10. Ten too many, but let us recognise the progress made.

The transformation in the economy has been enormous: unemployment at its lowest since 1975; long-term unemployment, down 65% since the agreement; manufacturing up 15%, uniquely in the UK.

New jobs, new investment and a new way of life, as anyone who walks through Belfast city centre, or that of Derry or any other town can see.

And in all sorts of small but immensely symbolic ways life has changed. Not for all, I know. If you're in the Short Strand, or the victim of the latest pipe bomb attack or caught in the intercommunity violence in north Belfast, these words about progress seem hollow. But actually the majority of people in Northern Ireland aren't mired in it.

I remember in the 1980s coming to lecture in Northern Ireland with a colleague at the Bar. I remember how we couldn't go to a pub but had to go to a secure club. I remember how our hosts—accountants, I think—looked under their cars each morning.

I remember at the airport being told about a terrorist incident a short distance away. I remember feeling when I was going there, I was going somewhere not just unsafe, but fundamentally different from any other part of the UK. Troops everywhere. Violence hanging over us as a cloud.

Northern Ireland is different today. Different and better. But not as it should and can be.

The disappointment comes not from the modesty of our achievements, which are considerable; but from the enormity of our expectations.

Unionist Insecurity

And all the way through, there has been one fundamental issue and I want to state it as I see it. I don't want on this occasion to be diplomatic. I think I have the duty and a right, from the very time I have spent on this issue, to give you my frank view.

For years nationalist Ireland felt treated as second-class citizens. Let me cross out the word "felt". They were treated as second-class citizens. Let us not even assign blame. But let us not deny fact. They wanted to be part of a united Ireland. They regarded the whole concept of Northern Ireland as a sectarian construct. They believed the only way to secure justice was to secure unification.

Unionism at the time was supreme but it was also suspicious. Suspicious that if it gave way to the demands of nationalism, it was a slippery slope leading to a united Ireland. Suspicious that the British government, of whatever colour, might say they were with them, but in reality would sell them out.

Today's Conservative opposition attack us over the Belfast agreement, calling us unprincipled, betraying unionism. But I recall yesterday's Conservative government, and Mrs [Margaret] Thatcher's Anglo-Irish agreement and later

Mr [John] Major's Downing Street declaration and the secret talks with the Irish Republican Army (IRA) even as the bombs exploded. But unionism recalls it all too. And it leads to suspicion and also to insecurity.

Insecure for all the reasons just given. Insecure because they believed they had as much right to be unionists as the nationalists had to be nationalist, but that the world sided with the nationalists. Insecure because the more they demonstrated the overt signs of their Britishness, the more different from the rest of the UK they seemed.

Republican Terrorism

And then into all this came the final and deadly ingredient of terrorism. I remember every year as a schoolboy spending my holidays in Ireland. Then one year, it all stopped.

It is hard for anyone to understand terrorism; and I do not believe it was ever or could ever be justified. But let us just reflect on its purposes. The purpose of republican terrorism was to create such a situation of chaos that Britain would give up on Northern Ireland. The purpose of loyalist terrorism was to retaliate, to dominate or to clear out Catholics.

For our part, the purpose of the British security response, often harsh, was to eliminate the violence as was our duty to do.

The fact is none of us succeeded in our purpose. The IRA were never going to bomb their way to a united Ireland and never could do so. I know the British people. They would simply never yield to it. The loyalists could not stand in the way of change. The British couldn't eliminate the IRA militarily. But one hangover from this history remains. Even when republicans realised they were not going to get Britain to give up Northern Ireland by terror, they still thought it had another tactical purpose. It gave them negotiating leverage. The British wouldn't give up Northern Ireland by terror but they might be forced by terror to negotiate, to take Northern Ireland seriously, to take the claims of nationalism seriously.

The prospect of a ceasefire was a sufficiently tantalising prospect, to make the British pay attention and to get real movement from unionism.

Working Out the Agreement

At the core of the agreement was this deal: in return for equality and justice—in politics, policing, in acceptance of nationalist identity—all parties were to commit exclusively to peace. And for unionism, the right of the people of Northern Ireland to remain part of the UK so long as a majority want to, was enshrined. Indeed, provided, in effect, unionists agreed to equality and to recognising the legitimacy of the identity of nationalists, the union would remain.

Of course, in working out the details, there were innumerable disputes over what equality, nationalist identity, the principle of consent meant in practice. This was one source of constant argument and disagreement, with the UK and Irish governments trying to negotiate a way through.

However, as time went on, it wasn't the main source. Increasingly, a different problem arose, and it is this that is at the heart of the present crisis.

Once the agreement was signed, republicans committed themselves to peace. But they had their suspicions too. They believed that if they relinquished entirely the paramilitary, they might find the new British enthusiasm for the political suddenly waned; that they could and would be safely ignored again.

So the game began. Negotiation after negotiation, a decommissioning act here, an IRA statement there, progress made but slowly. However, it all came with another price. The unionists, unsurprisingly, kept pointing out that the IRA still existed; that this was not an organisation committed to exclusively peaceful means; and that they, the unionists, were obliged to sit in government with its political wing.

So, rather than change being easier for unionists to embrace, and the British government to drive through, change became a trade: with the IRA, to get more movement over leaving violence behind; with the unionists to compensate them for their discomfort at the IRA's continuing existence. The result? A belief on both sides that the other is not sincere and the British government can't be trusted.

All the while, we were coming to a crunch point. Would republicanism really take the final step of committing exclusively, Sinn Fein and the IRA, to the peaceful path; or would they wait for the British finally to complete the normalisation of Northern Ireland, the policing and other changes promised, before doing so?

That is the crunch and the problem is that the very thing republicans used to think gave them negotiating leverage, doesn't do it anymore. It no longer acts to remove unionist intransigence, but to sustain it; it no longer pushes the British government forward, but delays us. It doesn't any longer justify [Ulster Union Party leader] David Trimble's engagement; it thwarts it.

I used to say we had to be sure all sides wanted the agreement to work. I am sure everyone does. Unionism, certainly as represented by David Trimble, does. I believe that. They know the past has to be laid to rest. In any event, even if some don't, the British government will simply not countenance any path other than implementing the agreement.

I also believe that Gerry Adams and Martin McGuinness [leaders of Sinn Fein, the IRA's political wing] want the agreement to work. I think they have taken huge risks to try to bury the past. That is not a fond hope. That is my considered judgement after four and a half years of the closest working with them.

But the crunch is the crunch. There is no parallel track left. The fork in the road has finally come. Whatever guarantees we need to give that we will implement the agreement, we will.

IRA Must End Violence

Whatever commitment to the end we all want to see, of a normalised Northern Ireland, I will make. But we cannot carry on with the IRA half in, half out of this process. Not just because it isn't right anymore. It won't work anymore.

Remove the threat of violence and the peace process is on an unstoppable path. That threat, no matter how damped down, is no longer reinforcing the political, it is actually destroying it. In fact, the continuing existence of the IRA as an active paramilitary organisation is now the best card those whom republicans call "rejectionist" unionists, have in their hand. It totally justifies their refusal to share power; it embarrasses moderate unionism and pushes wavering unionists into the hands of those who would just return Northern Ireland to the past. And because it also embarrasses the British and Irish governments, it makes it harder for us to respond to nationalist concerns. . . .

So: that's where we are. Not another impasse. But a fundamental choice of direction, a turning point. . . .

The People Want Peace

So: what do we have? We have a situation where, in truth, the overwhelming majority of people in Northern Ireland and their political leaders want to see the agreement implemented; want the institutions up and running again; accept the basic deal of justice for peace; but don't have the requisite trust to continue unless all the remaining bits of the puzzle are clear and fitted together.

Another inch-by-inch negotiation won't work. Symbolic gestures, important in their time, no longer build trust.

It's time for acts of completion. We will do our best to carry on implementing the agreement in any event. But, should real change occur, we can implement the rest of the agreement, including on normalisation, in its entirety and not in stages but together. And we are prepared to do what is necessary to protect the institutions against arbitrary interruption and interference. But that means also commitment from others. Unionism to make the institutions secure and stable. Nationalists to act if violence returns. Republicans to make the commitment to exclusively peaceful means, real, total and permanent. For all of us: an end to tolerance of paramilitary activity in any form. A decision that from here on in, a criminal act is a criminal act. One law for all, applied equally to all.

What has been interesting over the past few days has been not the comments of the politicians which, and I include ourselves, have been predictable; but the comments of people in the street. They have been genuinely sad that the executive and local decision-making has been suspended; genuinely understanding of why; and very clear that the only way forward is for the changes to be completed, not rolled back.

And, as ever, ordinary people who work by instinct and who change naturally in their views, are ahead of politics which too often works by reference to established tradition and hallowed positions that survive the passage of time and sentiment, and make change, even when obvious, hard to acknowledge. The time in which we live, has two characteristics amongst others that are common in the civilised world. Especially post–11 September, there is a complete hatred of terrorism. No democratic political process can yield to it. That's why, quite apart from anything else, the violence in Northern Ireland is pointless. It is just an obstruction to politics. And the second thing is a complete intolerance of injustice on the basis of race or sex or religion. That's not to say such injustice doesn't exist. It does. But it has no place in respectable politics. It's regarded as unacceptable. And that is in fact true today in Northern Ireland in a way it wasn't 30 years ago. People may worry about loss of cultural identity but they know the days of justifying discrimination are gone.

The Moment of Choice

In the end, justice for peace is in tune with our age. That's why this process in Northern Ireland despite it all, can still work.

Four-and-a-half years on, the way forward remains the same. The question is: do we have the courage as politicians to do what the people want us to do? Do we trust each other enough to make the acts of completion happen? I can only tell you as British prime minister that I have that trust in all the parties I have worked with.

Now is the moment of choice. The same standards must apply to all. And we must implement the agreement in full, because it is the choice of the people; the people here, the people in the south and the people of the United Kingdom as a whole. I honestly believe there is no other way.

Palestinian Terrorists Are Freedom Fighters

Yasser Arafat

Palestine, controlled since 1918 by the British, became
home to both native Arabs and to many Jewish refugees
fleeing persecution in Europe. After World War II, the
British decided to leave Palestine, and the United Nations
(UN) adopted a plan in 1947 calling for partition of
Palestine into Jewish and Arab states. Arabs fought the
establishment of a Jewish state, and the Arab-Jewish conflict has continued to the present day.

In 1965, the Palestine Liberation Organization (PLO)
was established to free Palestine from Israeli occupation,
and in 1968 Yasser Arafat became the leader of the PLO.
For decades the PLO launched bloody attacks on Israel,
and Arafat became known as a ruthless terrorist. On November 13, 1974, in a speech excerpted below, Arafat
made a dramatic appearance before the UN General Assembly and called on the world community to view the
PLO not as terrorists but as freedom fighters resisting Israeli occupation and oppression. The appearance of
Arafat before the UN was a diplomatic feat for the PLO
and a defeat for the United States and Israel, which had
fought to prevent the Palestinians from being recognized
as a people by the UN. The following year, 1975, the
United States finally recognized that the Palestinians had
legitimate interests that had to be considered as part of
an Arab-Israeli peace.

In 1988, the PLO agreed to recognize Israel as a sov-

Yasser Arafat, speech before the United Nations General Assembly, November 13,
1974.

ereign state, and in 1993, Arafat met with Israeli prime
minister Yitzhak Rabin and signed a peace agreement,
known as the Oslo Peace Accords, which gave Palestinians self-rule. As a result of the peace agreement, Arafat,
Rabin, and Israeli foreign minister Shimon Peres were
granted the 1994 Nobel Peace Prize, and in 1996, Arafat
was elected the first president of the Palestinian Council
governing the West Bank and the Gaza Strip.

In recent years, however, Arafat and the PLO have
lost credibility in world diplomatic circles. In 1999, Arafat
rejected a peace proposal from Israel that offered the
Palestinians a sovereign state with control over much of
the territory in the West Bank, but did not include
Jerusalem. Since then, the renewal of terrorist violence
against Israel, and increased terrorist activity by the more
radical Palestinian resistance groups, such as Hamas and
Hezbollah, have made it difficult for Arafat to exercise
significant clout on Palestinian issues. In 2002, Israel, under the leadership of Ariel Sharon, placed Arafat under
house arrest after he failed to stop continuing Palestinian
terrorist strikes against Israeli civilians. Although Israel's
targeting of Arafat has had the effect of increasing his status among Arabs, neither the PLO nor Israel have been effective in moving toward a resolution of the Palestinian-
Israeli conflict.

Mr. President, I thank you for having invited the
Palestine Liberation Organization to participate in
the plenary session of the United Nations General
Assembly. I am grateful to all those representatives of United
Nations member states who contributed to the decision to in-
troduce the question of Palestine as a separate item on the
Agenda of this Assembly. That decision made possible the
Assembly's resolution inviting us to address it on the ques-
tion of Palestine. . . .

The Jewish invasion of Palestine began in 1881. Before
the first large wave of settlers started arriving, Palestine had
a population of half a million, most of these Muslims or

Christians, and about 10,000 Jews. Every sector of the population enjoyed the religious tolerance characteristic of our civilization.

Palestine was then a verdant land, inhabited by an Arab people in the course of building its life and enriching its indigenous culture. Between 1882 and 1917 the Zionist movement settled approximately 50,000 European Jews in our homeland. To do that it resorted to trickery and deceit in order to plant them in our midst. Its success in getting Britain to issue the Balfour Declaration [letter from British foreign secretary Arthur James Balfour to Jewish leader Lord Rothschild indicating for the first time Britain's support for providing a homeland for the Jews in Palestine] demonstrated the alliance between Zionism and colonialism. Furthermore, by promising to the Zionist movement what was not hers to give, Britain showed how oppressive the rule of colonialism was. As it was then constituted, the League of Nations abandoned our Arab people, and [U.S. president Woodrow] Wilson's pledges and promises came to nought. In the guise of a mandate, British colonialism was cruelly and directly imposed upon us. The mandate document issued by the League of Nations was to enable the Zionist invaders to consolidate their gains in our homeland.

In thirty years the Zionist movement succeeded, in collaboration with its colonialist ally, in settling more European Jews on the land, thus usurping the properties of Palestinian Arabs.

By 1947 the number of Jews had reached 600,000; they owned less than 6 per cent of Palestinian arable land. The figure should be compared with the [Arab] population of Palestine, which at that time was 1,250,000.

The Creation of Israel by the UN

As a result of the collusion between the mandatory power and the Zionist movement and with the support of the United States, this General Assembly early in its history approved a recommendation to partition our Palestinian homeland. This took place on November 30, 1947, in an atmosphere of questionable actions and strong pressure. The General Assembly partitioned what it had no right to divide—an indivisible homeland. When we rejected that decision, our position corresponded to that of the real mother who refused to permit Solomon to cut her child in two when the other woman claimed the child as hers. Furthermore, even though the partition resolution granted the colonialist settlers 54 per cent of the land of Palestine, their dissatisfaction with the decision prompted them to wage a war of terror against the civilian Arab population. They occupied 81 per cent of the total area of Palestine, uprooting a million Arabs. Thus, they occupied 524 Arab towns and villages, of which they destroyed 385, completely obliterating them in the process. Having done so, they built their own settlements and colonies on the ruins of our farms and our groves. The roots of the Palestine question lie here. Its causes do not stem from any conflict between two religions or two nationalisms. Nor is it a border conflict between neighbouring states. It is the cause of people deprived of its homeland, dispersed and uprooted, the majority of whom live in exile and in refugee camps.

Israel's Aggression Against the Palestinians

With support from imperialist and colonialist powers, headed by the United States of America, this Zionist entity managed to get itself accepted as a United Nations member. It further succeeded in getting the Palestine question deleted from the Agenda of the United Nations and in deceiving world public opinion by presenting our cause as a problem of refugees in need either of charity from do-gooders, or settlement in a land not theirs.

Not satisfied with all this, the racist state, founded on the imperialist-colonialist concept, turned itself into a base of imperialism and into an arsenal of weapons. This enabled it to assume its role of subjugating the Arab people and of committing aggression against them, in order to satisfy its ambitions of further expansion in Palestinian and other Arab lands. In addition to the many instances of aggression committed by this entity against the Arab states, it has launched two large-scale wars, in 1956 and 1967, thereby endangering world peace and security.

As a result of Zionist aggression in June 1967, the enemy occupied Egyptian Sinai as far as the Suez Canal. The enemy occupied Syria's Golan Heights, in addition to all Palestinian land west of the Jordan. All these developments have led to the creation in our area of what has come to be known as the "Middle East Problem." The situation has been rendered more serious by the enemy's persistence in maintaining its unlawful occupation and in further consolidating it, thus establishing a beachhead for world imperialism's thrust against our Arab nation. All Security Council decisions and calls by world public opinion for withdrawal from the lands occupied in June 1967 have been ignored. Despite all the peaceful and diplomatic efforts on the international level, the enemy has not been deterred from his expansionist policy. The only alternative open to our Arab nations, chiefly Syria and Egypt, was to expend exhaustive efforts to prepare, firstly, to resist this barbarous armed invasion by force and, secondly, to liberate Arab lands and to restore the rights of the Palestinian people, after all other peaceful means had failed.

Under these circumstances, the fourth war broke out in October 1973, bringing home to the Zionist enemy the bankruptcy of its policy of occupation and expansion and its reliance on the concept of military might. Despite all this, the leaders of the Zionist entity are far from having learned any lesson from their experience. They are making preparations for the fifth war, resorting once more to the language of military superiority, aggression, terrorism, subjugation and, finally, always to war in their dealings with the Arabs. . . .

Palestinian Revolution Directed Against Zionism, Not Judaism

If the immigration of Jews to Palestine had had as its objective the goal of enabling them to live side by side with us, enjoying the same rights and assuming the same duties, we would have opened our doors to them, as far as our homeland's capacity for absorption permitted. Such was the case with the thousands of Armenians and Circassians who still live among us in equality as brethren and citizens. But no one can conceivably demand that we submit to or accept that the goal of this immigration should be to usurp our homeland, disperse our people, and turn us into second-class citizens. Therefore, since its inception, our revolution has not been motivated by racial or religious factors. Its target has never been the Jew, as a person, but racist Zionism and aggression. In this sense, ours is also a revolution for the Jew, as a human being. We are struggling so that Jews, Christians, and Muslims may live in equality, enjoying the same rights and assuming the same duties, free from racial or religious discrimination.

a) We distinguish between Judaism and Zionism. While we maintain our opposition to the colonialist Zionist movement, we respect the Jewish faith. Today, almost one century after the rise of the Zionist movement, we wish to warn of its increasing danger to the Jews of the world, to our Arab peoples and to world peace and security. For Zionism encourages the Jew to emigrate from his homeland and grants him an artificially-made nationality. The Zionists proceed with their destructive activities even though these have proved ineffective. The phenomenon of constant emigration from Israel, which is bound to grow as the bastions of colonialism and racism in the world fall, is an example of the inevitability of the failure of such activities.

b) We urge the people and governments of the world to stand firm against Zionist attempts at encouraging world Jewry to emigrate from their countries and to usurp our land. We urge them as well firmly to oppose any discrimination against any human being, as to religion, race, or colour.

c) Why should our people and our homeland be responsible for the problems of Jewish immigration, if such problems exist in the minds of some people? Why do the supporters of these problems not open their own countries, which are much bigger, to absorb and help these immigrants?

Palestinian Freedom Fighters Are Not Terrorists

Those who call us terrorists wish to prevent world public opinion from discovering the truth about us and from seeing the justice on our faces. They seek to hide the terrorism and tyranny of their acts, and our own posture of self-defence.

The difference between the revolutionary and the terrorist lies in the reason for which each fights. For whoever stands by a just cause and fights for the freedom and liberation of his land from invaders, settlers and colonialists would have been incorrectly called terrorist; the American people in their struggle for liberation from the British colonialists would have been terrorists, the European resistance against the Nazis would be terrorism, the struggle of the Asian, African and Latin American peoples would also be terrorism. It is actually a just and proper struggle of the Asian, African, and Latin American peoples, consecrated by the United Nations Charter and by the Declaration of Human Rights. As to those who fight against just causes, those who wage war to occupy the homelands of others, and to plunder, exploit and colonize their peoples—those are the people whose actions should be condemned, who should be called war criminals: for the just cause determines the right to struggle.

Israeli Zionists Are the True Terrorists

Zionist terrorism which was waged against the Palestinian people to evict them from their country and usurp their land is on record in your documents. Thousands of our people have been assassinated in their villages and towns; tens of thousands of others have been forced by rifle and artillery fire to leave their homes and the crops they have sown in the lands of their fathers. Time and time again our children, women and aged have been evicted and have had to wander in the deserts and climb mountains without any food or water. No one who in 1948 witnessed the catastrophe that befell the inhabitants of hundreds of villages and towns—in Jerusalem, Jaffa, Lydda, Ramleh, and Galilee—no one who has been a witness to that catastrophe will ever forget the experience, even though the mass blackout has succeeded in hiding these horrors as it has hidden the traces of 385 Palestinian villages and towns destroyed at the time and erased from the map. The destruction of 19,000 houses during the past seven years, which is equivalent to the complete destruction of 200 more

Palestinian villages, and the great number of maimed as a result of the treatment they were subjected to in Israeli prisons, cannot be hidden by any blackout. . . .

The small number of Palestinian Arabs whom the Zionists did not succeed in uprooting in 1948 are at present refugees in their own country. Israeli law treats them as second-class citizens . . . and they have been subject to all forms of racial discrimination and terror after the confiscation of their land and property. They have been victims of bloody massacres such as that of Kafr Qassim; they have been expelled from their villages and denied the right to return, as in the case of the inhabitants of Iqrit and Kafr Bir'im. For 26 years, our population has been living under martial law and has been denied freedom of movement without prior permission from the Israeli military governor—this at a time when an Israeli law was promulgated granting citizenship to any Jew anywhere who wanted to emigrate to our homeland. Moreover, another Israeli law stipulated that Palestinians who were not present in their villages or towns at the time they were occupied are not entitled to Israeli citizenship.

The record of Israeli rulers is replete with acts of terror perpetrated on those of our people who remained under occupation in Sinai and the Golan Heights. The criminal bombardment of the Bahr al-Baqar School and the Abu Za'bal factory in Egypt are but two such unforgettable acts of terrorism. The destruction of the Libyan aircraft is another unforgettable act. The total destruction of the city of Quneitra is yet another tangible instance of systematic terrorism. If a record of Zionist terrorism in south Lebanon were to be compiled, and this terrorism is still continuing, the enormity of its acts would shock even the most hardened: piracy, bombardments, scorched earth, destruction of hundreds of homes, eviction of civilians and the kidnapping of Lebanese citizens. This clearly constitutes a violation of Lebanese sovereignty and is in preparation for the diversion of the Litani River waters.

Need one remind this Assembly of the numerous resolutions adopted by it condemning Israeli aggressions committed against Arab countries, Israeli violations of human rights and the articles of the Geneva Conventions, as well as the resolutions pertaining to the annexation of the city of Jerusalem and its restoration to its former status? The only description for these acts is that they are acts of barbarism and terrorism. And yet, the Zionist racists and colonialists have the temerity to describe the just struggle of our people as terror. Could there be a more flagrant distortion of truth than this? We ask those who usurped our land, who are committing murderous acts of terrorism against our people and are practising racial discrimination more extensively than the racists of South Africa, we ask them to keep in mind the United Nations General Assembly resolution that called for the expulsion of South Africa from the United Nations. Such is the inevitable fate of every racist country that adopts the law of the jungle, usurps the homeland of others and oppresses its people.

The Palestinian Struggle for Self-Determination

For the past 30 years, our people have had to struggle against British occupation and Zionist invasion, both of which had one intention, namely the usurpation of our land. Six major revolts and tens of popular uprisings were stayed to foil these attempts, so that our homeland might remain ours. Over 30,000 martyrs, the equivalent in comparative terms of 6 million Americans, died in the process.

When the majority of the Palestinian people was uprooted from its homeland in 1948, the Palestinian struggle for self-determination continued in spite of efforts to destroy it. We tried every possible means to continue our political struggle to attain our national rights, but to no avail. Meanwhile we had to struggle for sheer existence. Even in exile we educated our children. This was all a part of trying to survive.

The Palestinian people have produced thousands of engineers, physicians, teachers and scientists who actively participated in the development of the Arab countries bordering on their usurped homeland. They have utilized their income to assist the young and aged amongst their people who could not leave the refugee camps. They have educated their younger brothers and sisters, have supported their parents and cared for their children. All along the Palestinian dreamt of return. Neither the Palestinian's allegiance to Palestine nor his determination to return waned; nothing could persuade him to relinquish his Palestinian identity or to forsake his homeland. The passage of time did not make him forget, as some hoped he would. When our people lost faith in the international community which persisted in ignoring its rights and when it became obvious that the Palestinians would not recoup one inch of Palestine through exclusively political means, our people had no choice but to resort to armed struggle. Into that struggle it poured its material and human resources and the flower of its youth. We bravely faced the most vicious acts of Israeli terrorism which were aimed at diverting our struggle and arresting it.

In the past ten years of our struggle, thousands of martyrs and twice as many wounded, maimed and imprisoned have been offered in sacrifice, all in an effort to resist the imminent threat of liquidation, to regain the right to self-determination and our right to return to our homeland. With the utmost dignity and the most admirable revolutionary spirit, our Palestinian people have not lost their spirit either in Israeli prisons and concentration camps or in the great prison of Israeli occupation. The people struggle for sheer existence and continue to strive to preserve the Arab character of the land. Thus they resist oppression, tyranny and terrorism in their grimmest forms.

It is through the armed revolution of our people that our political leadership and our national institutions finally crystallized and a national liberation movement, comprising all Palestinian factions, organizations and capabilities, materialized in the Palestine Liberation Organization.

The PLO Represents the Palestinian People

Through our militant Palestine national liberation movement, our people's struggle has matured and grown enough to accommodate political and social struggle in addition to armed struggle. The Palestine Liberation Organization has been a major factor in creating a new Palestinian individual, qualified to shape the future of our Palestine, not merely content with mobilizing the Palestinians for the challenges of the present. The Palestine Liberation Organization can be proud of having a large number of cultural and educational activities, even while engaged in armed struggle, and at a time when it faced the increasingly vicious blows of Zionist terrorism. We have established institutes for scientific research, agricultural development and social welfare, as well as centres for the revival of our cultural heritage and the preservation of our folklore. Many Palestinian poets, artists and writers have enriched Arab culture in particular, and world culture generally. Their profoundly humane works have won the admiration of all those familiar with them. In contrast to that, our enemy has been systematically destroying our culture and disseminating racist, colonialist ideologies; in short, everything that impedes progress, justice, democracy and peace.

The Palestine Liberation Organization has earned its legitimacy because of the sacrifice inherent in its pioneering role, and also because of its dedicated leadership of the struggle. It has also been granted this legitimacy by the Palestinian masses, which in harmony with it have chosen it to lead the struggle according to its directives. The Palestine Liberation Organization has also gained its legitimacy by representing every faction, union or group as well as every Palestinian talent, either in the National Council or in people's institutions. This legitimacy was further strengthened by the support of the entire Arab nation which supports it, and further consecrated during the last Arab Summit Conference, which affirmed the right of the Palestine Liberation Organization, in its capacity as the sole representative of the Palestinian people, to establish an independent national authority on all liberated Palestinian territory.

Moreover, the Palestine Liberation Organization's legitimacy has been intensified as a result of fraternal support given by other liberation movements and by friendly, like-minded nations that stood by our side, encouraging and aiding us in our struggle to secure our national rights. . . .

The Palestine Liberation Organization represents the Palestinian people. Because of this, the Palestine Liberation Organization expresses the wishes and hopes of its people. Because of this, too, it brings these very wishes and hopes before you, urging you not to shirk a momentous historic responsibility towards our just cause. . . .

Palestinian Dream of a Peaceful Palestine

I am a rebel and freedom is my cause. I know well that many of you present here today once stood in exactly the same position of resistance as I now occupy and from which I must fight. You once had to convert dreams into reality by your struggle. Therefore you must now share my dream. I think this is exactly why I can ask you now to help, as together we bring out our dream into a bright reality, our common dream for a peaceful future in Palestine's sacred land. . . .

Why therefore should I not dream and hope? For is not revolution the making real of dreams and hopes? So let us work together that my dream may be fulfilled, that I may return with any people out of exile, there in Palestine to live with this Jewish freedom-fighter and his partners, with this Arab priest and his brothers, in one democratic state where Christian, Jew and Muslim live in justice, equality, fraternity.

Is this not a noble goal and worthy of my struggle alongside all lovers of freedom everywhere? For the most admirable thing about this goal is that it is Palestinian, from the land of peace, the land of martyrdom, heroism, and history.

Let us remember that the Jews of Europe and here in the United States have been known to lead the struggles for secularism and the separation of church and state. They have also been known to fight against discrimination on religious grounds. How can they reject this humane and honourable programme for the Holy Land, the land of peace and equality? How can they continue to support the most fanatic, discriminatory and closed of nations in its policy?

In my capacity as Chairman of the Palestine Liberation Organization and commander of the Palestinian revolution I proclaim before you that when we speak of our common hopes for the Palestine of tomorrow we include in our perspective all Jews now living in Palestine who choose to live with us there in peace and without discrimination.

In my capacity as commander of the forces of the Palestine Liberation Organization I call upon Jews to turn away one by one from the illusory promises made to them by Zionist ideology and Israeli leadership. They are offering Jews perpetual bloodshed, endless war and continuous thraldom. We invite them to emerge into a more open realm of free choice, far from their present leadership's effects to implant in them a Masada complex and make it their destiny. We offer them the most generous solution—that we should live together in a framework of just peace in our democratic Palestine.

In my formal capacity as Chairman of the Palestine Liberation Organization I announce here that we do not wish one drop of either Jewish or Arab blood to be shed; neither do we delight in the continuation of killings for a single moment, once a just peace, based on our people's rights, hopes, and aspirations has been finally established.

In my capacity as Chairman of the Palestine Liberation Organization and commander of the Palestinian revolution I appeal to you to accompany our people in its struggle to attain its right to self-determination. This right is consecrated in the United Nations Charter and has been repeatedly confirmed in resolutions adopted by this august body since the drafting of the Charter. I appeal to you, further, to aid our people's return to its homeland from an involuntary exile imposed upon it by force of arms, by tyranny, by oppression, so that we may regain our property, our land, and thereafter live in our national homeland, free and sovereign, enjoying all the privileges of nationhood.

I appeal to you to enable our people to set up their national authority and establish their national entity in their own land.

Only then will our people be able to contribute all their energies and resources to the field of civilization and human creativity. Only then will they be able to protect their beloved Jerusalem and make it, as they have done for so many centuries, the shrine of all religions, free from all terrorism and coercion.

Today I have come bearing an olive branch and a freedom-fighter's gun. Do not let the olive branch fall from my hand. Do not let the olive branch fall from my hand. Do not let the olive branch fall from my hand.

Israel Must Fight to Win the War Against Palestinian Terror

Benjamin Netanyahu

In 1993, the PLO and Israel's prime minister Yitzhak Rabin negotiated a peace agreement known as the Oslo Peace Accords, which gave Palestinians self-rule and provided for further negotiations. Thereafter, Yasser Arafat was elected the first president of the Palestinian Council governing the West Bank and the Gaza Strip, and peace negotiations continued with Israel.

In 1995, Rabin was assassinated, and on June 18, 1996, right-wing Likud Party chairman Benjamin Netanyahu was sworn in as the new prime minister. During Netanyahu's tenure as prime minister, peace negotiations with the PLO slowed considerably. In 1998, however, Netanyahu and Arafat met and agreed on several important issues called for by the 1993 Oslo Peace Accords; the Palestinians agreed to remove language from their founding charter that called for destroying Israel, and Israel promised to withdraw from additional areas of the West Bank.

Following this meeting, Netanyahu was attacked by the right wing for giving up Israeli territory, leading him to later renege on the promise of Israeli withdrawals. Nevertheless, he was unable to shore up his political support, and in 1999, he was defeated by Labor Party leader Ehud Barak, who promised voters to revive the peace

Benjamin Netanyahu, speech before the U.S. Senate, Washington, DC, April 10, 2002.

process with the PLO. Barak followed through on his promise and met with Arafat in the famous Camp David peace talks in 1999, during which Barak offered the Palestinians a sovereign state with control over much of the territory in the West Bank, excluding Jerusalem. Arafat turned down the proposal, and Israelis again elected a right-wing conservative to the office of prime minister, Ariel Sharon, whose administration has pursued a hard-line military approach on Palestinian issues.

On April 10, 2002, in the speech below, Netanyahu spoke before the U.S. Senate, urging the United States to support Israel's fight against Palestinian terrorism. He protests the double standard that endorses America's war against terrorism but asks Israel to seek a political solution in response to Palestinian attacks. Israel must combat terrorism with the same determination that the United States has displayed in its antiterrorist efforts.

I have come here to voice what I believe is an urgently needed reminder: That the war on terror can be won with clarity and courage or lost with confusion and vacillation.

Principles on Terrorism Announced by President Bush

Seven months ago, on a clear day in the capital of freedom, I was given the opportunity to address you, the guardians of liberty. I will never forget that day—a day when words that will echo for ages pierced the conscience of the free world: Words that lifted the spirits of an American nation that had been savagely attacked by evil. Words that looked that evil straight in the eye and boldly declared that it would be utterly destroyed. Most important, words that charted a bold course for victory. Those words were not mine. They were the words of the President of the United States.

In an historic speech to the world last September [2001] and with determined action in the crucial months that followed, President Bush and his administration outlined a vision that had the moral and strategic clarity necessary to win the war on terror. The moral clarity emanated from an iron-clad definition of terror and an impregnable moral truth. Terrorism was understood to be the deliberate targeting of civilians in order to achieve political ends. And it was always unjustifiable. With a few powerful words, President Bush said all that needed to be said: 'Terrorism is never justified.'

The strategic clarity emanated from the recognition that international terrorism depends on the support of sovereign states, and that fighting it demands that these regimes be either deterred or dismantled. In one clear sentence, President Bush expressed this principle: 'No distinction will be made between the terrorists and the regimes that harbor them.'

This moral and strategic clarity was applied with devastating effect to the Taliban regime in Afghanistan that supported Al Qaeda terrorism. No false moral equivalence was drawn between the thousands of Afghan civilians who were the unintentional casualties of America's just war and the thousands of American civilians deliberately targeted on September 11. No strategic confusion led America to pursue Al Qaeda terrorists while leaving the Taliban regime in place.

Soon after the war began, the American victory over the forces of terror in Afghanistan brought to light the third principle in the war on terror—namely, that the best way to defeat terror is to defeat it. At first, this seemingly trite observation was not fully understood. Contrary to popular belief, the motivating force behind terror is neither desperation nor destitution. It is hope—the hope of terrorists systematically brainwashed by the ideologues who manipulate them that their savagery will break the will of their enemies and help them achieve their objectives—political, religious, or otherwise. Defeat this hope and you defeat terrorism. Convince terrorists, their sponsors, and potential new recruits that terrorism will be thoroughly uprooted and severely punished and you will stop it cold in its tracks.

By adhering to these three principles—moral clarity, strategic clarity and the imperative of victory—the forces of freedom, led by America, are well on their way to victory against terror from Afghanistan.

But that is only the first step in dismantling the global terrorist network. The other terrorist regimes must now be rapidly dealt with in similar fashion. Yet today, just seven months into the war, it is far from certain that this will be done. Faced with the quintessential terrorist regime of our time—a regime that both harbors and perpetrates terror on an unimaginable scale—the free world is muddling its principles, losing its nerve, and thereby endangering the successful prosecution of this war. The question many in my country are now asking is this: Will America apply its principles consistently and win this war, or will it selectively abandon those principles and thereby ultimately lose the war?

My countrymen ask this question because they believe that terrorism is an indivisible evil and that the war against terror must be fought indivisibly. They believe that if moral clarity is obfuscated, or if you allow one part of the terror network to survive, much less be rewarded for its crimes, then the forces of terror will regroup and rise again. Until last week, I was certain that the United States would adhere to its principles and lead the free world to a decisive victory. Today, I too have my concerns.

I am concerned that when it comes to terror directed against Israel, the moral and strategic clarity that is so crucial for victory is being twisted beyond recognition. I am concerned that the imperative of defeating terror everywhere is being ignored when the main engine of Palestinian terror is allowed to remain intact.

My concern deepened when, incredibly, Israel was asked to stop fighting terror and return to a negotiating table with a regime that is committed to the destruction of the Jewish State and openly embraces terror. Yasser Arafat brazenly pursues an ideology of policide—the destruction of a state—and meticulously promotes a cult of suicide. With total control of the media, the schools, and ghoulish kindergarten camps for children that glorifies suicide martyrdom, Arafat's dictatorship has indoctrinated a generation of Palestinians in a culture of death, producing waves of human bombs that massacre Jews in buses, discos, supermarkets, pizza shops, cafés—everywhere and anywhere.

Israel has not experienced a terrorist attack like the one the world witnessed on that horrific day in September. That unprecedented act of barbarism will never be forgotten. But in the last eighteen months, Israel's six million citizens have buried over four hundred victims of terror—a per capita toll equivalent to half a dozen September 11ths. This daily, hourly carnage is also unprecedented in terrorism's bloody history. Yet at the very moment when support for Israel's war against terror should be stronger than ever, my nation is being asked to stop fighting.

Though we are assured by friends that we have the right to defend ourselves, we are effectively asked not to exercise that right. I am concerned that the State of Israel, that has for decades bravely manned the front lines against terror, is being pressed to back down just when it is on the verge of uprooting Palestinian terror.

These concerns first surfaced with the appearance of a reprehensible moral symmetry that equates Israel, a democratic government that is defending itself against terror, with the Palestinian dictatorship that is perpetrating it. The deliberate targeting of Israeli civilians is shamefully equated with the unintentional loss of Palestinian life that is the tragic but unavoidable consequence of legitimate warfare. Worse, since Palestinian terrorists both deliberately target civilians and hide behind them, Israel is cast as the guilty party because more Palestinians have been killed in Arafat's terrorist war than Israelis.

No one, of course, would dare suggest that the United States was the guilty party in World War II because German casualties, which included millions of civilians, were twenty times higher then American casualties. So too, only a twisted and corrupt logic would paint America and Britain as the aggressors in the current war because Afghan casualties are reported to have well exceeded the death toll of September 11. But our friends should have no illusions. With or without international support, the government of Israel must fight not only to defend its people, restore a dangerously eroded deterrence and secure the Jewish State, but also to ensure that the free world wins the war against terror in this pivotal arena in the heart of the Middle East.

Israel must now do three things. First, it must dismantle Arafat's terrorist regime and expel Arafat from the region. As long as the engineer of Palestinian terror remains in the territories, terror will never stop and the promise of peace will never be realized. Second, Israel must clean out terrorists, weapons, and explosives from all Palestinian controlled areas. No place, whether it is a refugee camp in Gaza or an office in Ramallah can be allowed to remain a haven for terror. Third, Israel must establish physical barriers separating the main Palestinian population centers from Israeli towns and cities. This will prevent any residual terrorists from reaching Israel. Done together, these three measures will dramatically reduce terrorism, bring security to the people of Israel and restore stability to the region.

Last week, the government of Israel began to take the second of these vital steps. Rather than bomb Palestinian populated cities and towns from the air—an operation that would have claimed thousands of civilian casualties—the Israeli army is taking on greater risk by using ground forces that painstakingly make their way through the hornet's nests of Palestinian terror. But instead of praising Israel for seeking to minimize civilian casualties through careful and deliberate action, most of the world's governments shamelessly condemn it.

No Political Solution to Terror

For seven months, many of these governments have rightly supported the war against Afghan terror. Yet after only seven days, their patience for the war against Palestinian terror ran out. The explanations that are offered for this double standard are not convincing. First it is said that war on Palestinian terror is different because a political process exists that can restore security and advance peace. This is not so. There can never be a political solution for terror. The grievance of terrorists can never be redressed through diplomacy. That will only encourage more terror.

Yasser Arafat's terrorist regime must be toppled, not courted. The Oslo agreements are dead. Yasser Arafat killed them. He tore it to shreds and soaked it in Jewish blood by violating every one of its provisions, including the two core commitments he made at Oslo: to recognize the State of Israel and to permanently renounce terrorism. With such a regime and such failure of leadership, no political process is possible. In fact, a political process can only begin when this terrorist regime is dismantled.

Israel and the War Against Iraq

Second, it is said that waging war on Palestinian terror today will destabilize the region and cripple the imminent war against Sadaam Hussein. This concern is also misplaced. Clearly, the urgent need to topple Sadaam is paramount. The commitment of America and Britain to dismantle this terrorist dictatorship before it obtains nuclear weapons deserves the unconditional support of all sane governments. But contrary to conventional wisdom, what has destabilized the region is not Israeli action against Palestinian terror, but rather, the constant pressure exerted on Israel to show restraint.

It is precisely the exceptional restraint shown by Israel for over a year and a half that has unwittingly emboldened its enemies and inadvertently increased the threat of a wider conflict. If Israeli restraint were to continue, the thousands that are now clamoring for war in Arab capitals will turn into millions, and an avoidable war will become inevitable. Half-measures against terrorists will leave their grievances intact, fueled by the hope of future victory. Full-measures will not redress those grievances, but it will convince them that pursuing terror is a prescription for certain defeat.

America must show that it will not heed the international call to stop Israel from exercising its right to defend itself. If America compromises its principles and joins in the chorus of those who demand that Israel disengage, the war on terror will be undermined. For if the world begins to believe that America may deviate from its principles, then terrorist regimes that might have otherwise been deterred will not be deterred. Those that might have crumbled under the weight of American resolve will not crumble. As a result, winning the war will prove far more difficult, perhaps impossible.

But my friends, I must also tell you that the charge that Israel, of all countries, is hindering the war against Sadaam is woefully unjust. For my country has done more than any other to make victory over Sadaam possible. Twenty-one years ago, Prime Minister Menachem Begin sent the Israeli air force on a predawn raid hundreds of miles away on one of the most dangerous military missions in our nation's history. When our pilots returned, we had successfully destroyed Sadaam's atomic bomb factory and crippled his capacity to build nuclear weapons. Israel was safer—and so was the world. But rather than thanking us for safeguarding freedom, the entire world condemned us. Ten years later, when American troops expelled Iraqi forces in the Gulf War, then secretary of Defense Richard Cheney expressed a debt of gratitude to Israel for the bold and determined action a decade earlier that had made victory possible.

Indeed, I am confident that in time those who would condemn Israel now will understand that rooting out Palestinian terror today will also make both Israel and the world safer tomorrow. For if we do not immediately shut down the terror factories where Arafat is producing human bombs, it is only a matter of time before suicide bombers will terrorize your cities. If not destroyed, this madness will strike in your buses, in your supermarkets, in your pizza parlors, in your cafés. Eventually, these human bombs will supplement their murderous force with suitcases equipped with devices of mass death that could make the horrors of September 11 pale by comparison. That is why there is no alternative to winning this war without delay. No part of the terrorist network can be left intact. For if not fully eradicated, like the most malignant cancer, it will regroup and attack again with even greater ferocity. Only by dismantling the entire network will we be assured of victory.

Terror Must Be Supplanted by Democracy

But to assure that this evil does not reemerge a decade or two from now, we must not merely uproot terror, but also plant the seeds of freedom. Because only under tyranny can a diseased totalitarian mindset be widely cultivated. This totalitarian mindset, which is essential for terrorists to suspend the normal rules that govern a man's conscience and prevents him from committing these grisly acts, does not breed in a climate of democracy and freedom. The open debate and plurality of ideas that buttress all genuine democracies and the respect for human rights and the sanctity of life that are the shared values of all free societies are a permanent antidote to the poison that the sponsors of terror seek to inject into the minds of their recruits. That is why it is also imperative that once the terrorist regimes in the Middle East are swept away, the free world, led by America, must begin to build democracy in their place.

We simply can no longer afford to allow this region to remain cloistered by a fanatic militancy. We must let the winds of freedom and independence finally penetrate the one region in the world that clings to unreformed tyranny. That in exercising our basic right to defend ourselves Israel is condemned by Arab dictatorships is predictable. That today a Europe which sixty years ago refused to lift a finger to save millions of Jews has turned its collective back on the Jewish State is downright shameful. But my friends, I must admit. I expected no better from them.

Yet the America I know has always been different. History has entrusted this nation with carrying the torch of freedom. And time and time again, through both war and peace, America has carried that torch with courage and with honor, combining a might the world has never known with a sense of justice that no power in history has possessed.

I have come before you today to ask you to continue to courageously and honorably carry that torch by standing by an outpost of freedom that is resisting an unprecedented terrorist assault. I ask you to stand by Israel's side in its fight against Arafat's tyranny of terror, and thereby help defeat an evil that threatens all of mankind.

The Libyan Revolution Begins

Muammar Qaddafi

Libya, originally part of the Ottoman Empire, was later colonized by Italy, and then occupied by Britain and France during World War II. In November 1949, the United Nations declared that Libya would be granted independence by January 1, 1952. Thereafter, however, the country was governed by a monarchy that remained dependent on British and U.S. economic support. In 1959, oil was discovered in Libya. Also, in the 1960s Arab nationalism began sweeping the Arab world.

On September 1, 1969, a group of military officers under the lead of Muammar Qaddafi launched an almost bloodless coup, toppling the monarchy. In a speech broadcast over Libyan radio that day, reprinted here, Qaddafi announced the beginning of his revolution and promised to create a just and prosperous society. Instead, throughout the 1970s and 1980s, Qaddafi used Libya's formidable oil resources to spread an anti-imperialist, revolutionary message around the world. He became one of the world's most well-known anti-West terrorists, carrying out numerous terrorist attacks and supporting other international terrorist groups, including the Irish Republican Army (IRA), Palestinian groups, Basque separatists, and others.

In what would become the most infamous terrorist act tied to Qaddafi's regime, in September 1988 a Pan American airliner blew up over Lockerbie, Scotland, killing 280 people. An investigation conducted by the United States and Britain concluded that two Libyan sus-

Muammar Qaddafi, speech broadcast over Libyan radio, September 1, 1969.

pects were responsible for the bombing—Abel Basset Ail Al-Maghrahi and Laman Khalifa Fhimah. In 1992, the UN imposed economic sanctions on Libya for its refusal to turn over the Lockerbie suspects; these sanctions effectively limited Qaddafi's ability to export terror. Finally, in 1999, Libya finally agreed to hand over Al-Maghrahi and Fhimah, allowing a suspension of the sanctions against Libya.

People of Libya! In response to your own will, fulfilling your most heartfelt wishes, answering your incessant demands for change and regeneration and your longing to strive towards these ends; listening to your incitement to rebel, your armed forces have undertaken the overthrow of the reactionary and corrupt regime, the stench of which has sickened and horrified us all. At a single blow your gallant army has toppled these idols and has destroyed their images. By a single stroke it has lightened the long dark night in which the Turkish domination was followed first by Italian rule, then by this reactionary and decadent regime, which was no more than a hot-bed of extortion, faction, treachery and treason.

The Libyan Arab Republic

From this day forward, Libya is a free, self-governing republic. She will adopt the name of The Libyan Arab Republic and will, by the grace of God, begin her task. She will advance on the road to freedom, the path of unity and social justice, guaranteeing equality to all her citizens and throwing wide in front of them the gates of honest employment, where injustice and exploitation will be banished, where no one will count himself master or servant, and where all will be free, brothers within a society in which, with God's help, prosperity and equality will be seen to rule us all.

Give us your hands. Open up your hearts to us. Forget past misfortunes, and, as one people, prepare to face the enemies of Islam, the enemies of humanity, those who have burned our sanctuaries and mocked at our honour. Thus shall we re-build our glory, we shall resurrect our heritage, we shall avenge our wounded dignity, and restore the rights which have been wrested from us.

You who have witnessed the sacred struggle of our hero, Omar al-Mukhtar [Libyan hero who fought against Italian occupation in the 1920s], for Libya, Arabism and Islam . . . You who have fought at the side of Ahmed al-Sherif [Libyan leader of Italian resistance during the 1910s] for a true ideal; you, sons of the desert and of our ancient cities, of our green countryside, and of our lovely villages,—onwards! For we have work to do! And the hour is come!

Foreign Friends Should Not Fear

On this occasion I have pleasure in assuring all our foreign friends that they need have no fears either for their property or for their safety; they are under the protection of our armed forces. And I would add, moreover, that our enterprise is in no sense directed against any state whatever, nor against international agreements or recognised international law. This is a purely internal affair concerning Libya and her problems alone.

Forward, then, and may peace be with you.

States That Support Terror Form an International "Murder, Incorporated"

Ronald Reagan

During the administration of President Ronald Reagan in the 1980s, the United States experienced a number of terrorist attacks on American citizens and American military and other institutions around the world. Indeed, the Reagan administration began with a focus on terrorism. In 1979, one year prior to Reagan's election, the Islamic Revolution in Iran had led to the capture of fifty-three American hostages at the U.S. embassy in Tehran. The failure of Reagan's predecessor, President Jimmy Carter, to gain the hostages' release is considered a large factor in Reagan's election.

In 1982, Iran helped to establish and finance a terrorist group in Lebanon, called Hezbollah, which fought against Israel's occupation of Beirut and attacked American diplomats and military stationed there. In 1983, for example, Hezbollah suicide bombers destroyed the American Embassy in Beirut, killing 60 people, as well as the U.S. Marine compound in Beirut, killing 241 people. Also during this time, Libyan dictator Muammar Qaddafi actively supported various terrorist groups worldwide and conducted terrorist attacks on American and British targets.

Ronald Reagan, speech to the American Bar Association, July 8, 1985.

In a July 8, 1985, speech to the American Bar Association, excerpted here, Reagan decried the increase in international terrorism and accused Iran, Libya, and several other nations (specifically, North Korea, Cuba, and Nicaragua) of forming a "Murder, Incorporated"—a core group of nations that train terrorists and support terrorist acts against the United States. Years later, in 2002, U.S. President George W. Bush made a similar accusation when he charged that Iran, Iraq, and North Korea form an "axis of evil" because they support terror and are seeking to develop weapons of mass destruction.

I'm delighted to be able to speak today, not just to the largest voluntary professional association in the world [the American Bar Association] but one whose exclusive concern is the starting point for any free society, a concern that is at the heart of civilized life: the law—our courts and legal system—justice itself.

Now, I want to be very candid with you this morning and tell you I'd been planning to come here today to speak on a number of legal issues . . . But I'm afraid this discussion will now have to wait for another occasion, for it's been overtaken by events of an international nature, events that I feel compelled as President to comment on today. . . . The reason we haven't had time to discuss the issues that I'd originally hoped to address this morning has to do with our hostages and what all of America have been through during recent weeks. Yet my purpose today goes even beyond our concern over the recent outrages in Beirut, El Salvador or the Air India tragedy, the Narita bombing or the Jordanian Airlines hijacking. We must look beyond these events because I feel it is vital not to allow them—as terrible as they are—to obscure an even larger and darker terrorist menace.

A Pattern of Terrorism

There is a temptation to see the terrorist act as simply the erratic work of a small group of fanatics. We make this mistake at great peril, for the attacks on America, her citizens, her allies, and other democratic nations in recent years do form a pattern of terrorism that has strategic implications and political goals. And only by moving our focus from the tactical to the strategic perspective, only by identifying the pattern of terror and those behind it, can we hope to put into force a strategy to deal with it.

So, let us go to the facts. Here is what we know: In recent years, there's been a steady and escalating pattern of terrorist acts against the United States and our allies and Third World nations friendly toward our interests. The number of terrorist acts rose from about 500 in 1983 to over 600 in 1984. There were 305 bombings alone last year [1984]—that works out to an average of almost one a day. And some of the most vicious attacks were directed at Americans or United States property and installations. And this pattern has continued throughout 1985, and in most cases innocent civilians are the victims of the violence. At the current rate, as many as 1,000 acts of terrorism will occur in 1985. Now, that's what we face unless civilized nations act together to end this assault on humanity.

In recent years, the Mideast has been one principal point of focus for these attacks—attacks directed at the United States, Israel, France, Jordan, and the United Kingdom. Beginning in the summer of 1984 and culminating in January and February of this year, there was also a series of apparently coordinated attacks and assassinations by left-wing terrorist groups in Belgium, West Germany, and France—attacks directed against American and NATO installations or military and industrial officials of those nations.

Now, what do we know about the sources of those attacks and the whole pattern of terrorist assaults in recent years? Well, in 1983 alone, the Central Intelligence Agency either confirmed or found strong evidence of Iranian involvement in 57 terrorist attacks. While most of these attacks occurred in Lebanon, an increase in activity by terrorists sympathetic to Iran was seen throughout Europe. Spain and France have seen such incidents, and in Italy seven pro-Iranian Lebanese students were arrested for plotting an attack on the U.S. Embassy, and this violence continues.

It will not surprise any of you to know that, in addition to Iran, we have identified another nation, Libya, as deeply involved in terrorism. We have evidence which links Libyan agents or surrogates to at least 25 incidents last year. Colonel [Muammar] Qadhafi's outrages against civilized conduct are, of course, as infamous as those of the Ayatollah Khomeini. The gunning down last year—from inside the Libyan Embassy—of a British policewoman is only one of many examples.

Since September 1984, Iranian-backed terrorist groups have been responsible for almost 30 attacks, and most recently, the Egyptian Government aborted a Libyan-backed plot to bomb our Embassy in Cairo. It was this pattern of state-approved assassination and terrorism by Libya that led the United States a few years ago to expel Libyan diplomats and has forced other nations to take similar steps since then. But let us, in acknowledging his commitment to terrorism, at least give Colonel Qadhafi his due. The man is candid. He said recently that Libya was—and I quote—"capable of exporting terrorism to the heart of America. We are also capable of physical liquidation and destruction and arson inside America."

And, by the way, it's important to note here that the recognition of this deep and ongoing involvement of Iran and Libya in international terrorism is hardly confined to our own government. Most police forces in Europe now take this involvement for granted, and this is not even to mention the warnings issued by world leaders. For example, the Jordanian leadership has publicly noted that Libyan actions caused the destruction of the Jordanian Embassy in Tripoli.

North Korea, Cuba, and Nicaragua

Now, three other governments, along with Iran and Libya, are actively supporting a campaign of international terrorism against the United States, her allies, and moderate Third World states.

First, North Korea. The extent and crudity of North Korean violence against the United States and our ally, South Korea, are a matter of record. Our aircraft have been shot down; our servicemen have been murdered in border incidents; and 2 years ago, four members of the South Korean Cabinet were blown up in a bombing in Burma by North Korean terrorists—a failed attempt to assassinate President Chun. This incident was just one more of an unending series of attacks directed against the Republic of Korea by North Korea.

Now, what is not readily known or understood is North Korea's wider links to the international terrorist network. There isn't time today to recount all of North Korea's efforts to foster separatism, violence, and subversion in other lands well beyond its immediate borders. But to cite one example, North Korea's efforts to spread separatism and terrorism in the free and prosperous nation of Sri Lanka are a deep and continuing source of tension in south Asia. And this is not even to mention North Korea's involvement here in our own hemisphere, including a secret arms agreement with the former Communist government in Grenada. I will also have something to say about North Korea's involvement in Central America in a moment.

And then there is Cuba, a nation whose government has, since the 1960's, openly armed, trained, and directed terrorists operating on at least three continents. This has occurred in Latin America. The OAS has repeatedly passed sanctions against Castro for sponsoring terrorism in places and countries too numerous to mention. This has also occurred in Africa. President Carter openly accused the Castro government of supporting and training Katangan terrorists from Angola in their attacks on Zaire. And even in the Middle East, Castro himself has acknowledged that he actively assisted the Sandinistas in the early seventies when they were training in the Middle East with terrorist factions of the PLO.

And finally there is the latest partner of Iran, Libya, North Korea, and Cuba in a campaign of international terror—the Communist regime in Nicaragua. The Sandinistas not only sponsor terror in El Salvador, Costa Rica, and Honduras—terror that led recently to the murder of four United States marines, two civilians, and seven Latin Americans— they provide one of the world's principal refuges for international terrorists.

Members of the Italian Government have openly charged that Nicaragua is harboring some of Italy's worst terrorists. And when we have evidence that in addition to Italy's Red

Brigades other elements of the world's most vicious terrorist groups—West Germany's Baader-Meinhoff Gang, the Basque ETA, the PLO, the Tupamaros, and the IRA—have found a haven in Nicaragua and support from that country's Communist dictatorship. In fact, the Communist regime in Nicaragua has made itself a focal point for the terrorist network and a case study in the extent of its scope.

Consider for just a moment that in addition to establishing strong international alliances with Cuba and Libya, including the receipt of enormous amounts of arms and ammunition, the Sandinistas are also receiving extensive assistance from North Korea. Nor are they reluctant to acknowledge their debt to the government of North Korea dictator Kim Il-song. Both Daniel and Humberto Ortega have recently paid official and state visits to North Korea to seek additional assistance and more formal relations. So, we see the Nicaraguans tied to Cuba, Libya, and North Korea. And that leaves only Iran. What about ties to Iran? Well, yes, only recently the Prime Minister of Iran visited Nicaragua bearing expressions of solidarity from the Ayatollah for the Sandinista Communists.

Murder, Incorporated

Now, I spoke a moment ago about the strategic goals that are motivating these terrorist states. In a minute I will add some comments of my own, but for the moment why don't we let the leaders of these outlaw governments speak for themselves about their objectives. During his state visit to North Korea, Nicaragua's Sandinista leader, Daniel Ortega, heard Kim Il-song say this about the mutual objectives of North Korea and Nicaragua: "If the peoples of the revolutionary countries of the world put pressure on and deal blows at United States imperialism in all places where it stretches its talons of aggression, they will make it powerless and impossible to behave as dominator any longer." And Colonel Qadhafi, who has a formal alliance with North Korea, echoed Kim Il-song's words when he laid out the agenda for the terrorist network: "We must force America to fight on a hundred fronts all over the Earth. We must force it to fight in Lebanon, to fight in

Chad, to fight in Sudan, and to fight in El Salvador."

So, there we have it—Iran, Libya, North Korea, Cuba, Nicaragua—continents away, tens of thousands of miles apart, but the same goals and objectives. I submit to you that the growth in terrorism in recent years results from the increasing involvement of these states in terrorism in every region of the world. This is terrorism that is part of a pattern, the work of a confederation of terrorist states. Most of the terrorists who are kidnaping and murdering American citizens and attacking American installations are being trained, financed, and directly or indirectly controlled by a core group of radical and totalitarian governments—a new, international version of Murder, Incorporated. And all of these states are united by one simple criminal phenomenon—their fanatical hatred of the United States, our people, our way of life, our international stature.

And the strategic purpose behind the terrorism sponsored by these outlaw states is clear: to disorient the United States, to disrupt or alter our foreign policy, to sow discord between ourselves and our allies, to frighten friendly Third World nations working with us for peaceful settlements of regional conflicts, and, finally, to remove American influence from those areas of the world where we're working to bring stable and democratic government; in short, to cause us to retreat, retrench, to become Fortress America.

Yes, their real goal is to expel America from the world. And that is the reason these terrorist nations are arming, training, and supporting attacks against this nation. And that is why we can be clear on one point: these terrorist states are now engaged in acts of war against the Government and people of the United States. And under international law, any state which is the victim of acts of war has the right to defend itself.

American People Will Not Tolerate Terror

Now, for the benefit of these outlaw governments who are sponsoring international terrorism against our nation, I'm prepared to offer a brief lesson in American history. A number of times in America's past, foreign tyrants, warlords, and totalitarian dictators have misinterpreted the well-known likeability, patience, and generosity of the American people as signs of weakness or even decadence. Well, it's true; we are an easygoing people, slow to wrath, hesitant to see danger looming over every horizon. But it's also true that when the emotions of the American people are aroused, when their patriotism and their anger are triggered, there are no limits to their national valor nor their consuming passion to protect this nation's cherished tradition of freedom. Teddy Roosevelt once put it this way: "The American people are slow to wrath, but when the wrath is once kindled it burns like a consuming flame." And it was another leader, this time a foreign adversary, Admiral [Isoroku] Yamamoto, who warned his own nation after its attack on Pearl Harbor that he feared "we have only awakened a sleeping giant and his reaction will be terrible."

Yes, we Americans have our disagreements, sometimes noisy ones, almost always in public—that's the nature of our open society—but no foreign power should mistake disagreement for disunity. Those who are tempted to do so should reflect on our national character and our history—a history littered with the wreckage of regimes who made the mistake of underestimating the vigor and will of the American people.

So, let me today speak for a united people. Let me say simply: We're Americans. We love this country. We love what she stands for, and we will always defend her. . . . We live for freedom—our own, our children's—and we will always stand ready to sacrifice for that freedom.

So, the American people are not—I repeat—not going to tolerate intimidation, terror, and outright acts of war against this nation and its people. And we're especially not going to tolerate these attacks from outlaw states run by the strangest collection of misfits, loony tunes, and squalid criminals since the advent of the Third Reich. . . .

But there's another point that needs to be made here, the point I made at the start of this discussion: that in taking a strategic—not just a tactical—view of terrorism, we must understand that the greatest hope the terrorists and their sup-

porters harbor, the very reason for their cruelty and vicious-
ness of their tactics, is to disorient the American people, to
cause disunity, to disrupt or alter our foreign policy, to keep
us from the steady pursuit of our strategic interests, to distract
us from our very real hope that someday the nightmare of totalitarian rule will end and self-government and personal freedom will become the birthright of every people on Earth.

And here, my fellow Americans, is where we find the real
motive behind the rabid and increasing anti-Americanism of
the international terrorist network. I've been saying for some
years now that the cause of totalitarian ideology is on the
wane; that all across the world there is an uprising of mind
and will, a tidal wave of longing for freedom and self-rule.
Well, no one senses this better than those who now stand
atop totalitarian states, especially those nations on the outer
periphery of the totalitarian world like Iran, Libya, North
Korea, Cuba, and Nicaragua. Their rulers are frightened;
they know that freedom is on the march and when it tri-
umphs their time in power is over.

You see, it's true that totalitarian governments are very
powerful and, over the short term, may be better organized
than the democracies. But it's also true—and no one knows
this better than totalitarian rulers themselves—that these
regimes are weak in a way that no democracy can ever be
weak. For the fragility of totalitarian government is the
fragility of any regime whose hold on its people is limited to
the instruments of police-state repression. That's why the
stakes are so high and why we must persevere. Freedom itself
is the issue—our own and the entire world's. Yes, America is
still a symbol to a few, a symbol that is feared and hated, but
to more, many millions more, a symbol that is loved, a country that remains a shining city on a hill.

Spain Condemns Basque Separatist Terrorism

Juan Miguel Linan Macias

The Basques are a sect living mostly in northern Spain but also parts of southwest France, with a culture and language separate from both the Spanish and French. When the dictator Francisco Franco came to power in Spain in 1939, he tried to unite Spain by banning the Basque language and forcibly integrating the Basques into Spanish society. The Basque people rebelled and sought an independent Basque state. The Euskadi Ta Askatasuna (ETA), which means "Basque Fatherland and Liberty," was formed in 1959 to fight for independence. Since that time, the group has engaged in terrorist acts against officials and property in Spain, including the assassination of Franco's successor, Admiral Luis Carrero Blanco.

Franco's death in 1975 restored democracy to Spain and granted considerable autonomy to the Basque region, creating a separate Basque parliament with control over local issues. This action satisfied the majority of Basque people; a small minority, however, have continued the ETA terrorist campaign. With the support of the overwhelming majority in Spain who reject the separatist violence, the Spanish government has reacted strongly to ETA terrorism. In 1997 the government sentenced all twenty-three members of the ETA's political wing to seven years imprisonment.

In 1998, a weakened ETA declared a cease-fire in order to pursue negotiations with the Spanish government.

Juan Miguel Linan Macias, speech before a NATO seminar on terrorism, Warsaw, Poland, February 22, 2002.

After fourteen months, however, the group resumed its terror strikes, killing Ernest Lluch, a former government minister, on November 21, 2000. Since then, the ETA violence has continued, as has the Spanish government's struggle to control it. In a speech given February 22, 2002, a representative from Spain's Ministry of Defense, Juan Miguel Linan Macias, outlines the history of Basque terrorism and the country's efforts to end the violence.

ETA's [Euskadi Ta Askatasuna] goal is the creation of a Basque independent state based on Marxist-Leninist principles. To this aim, it seeks the separation of the three Basque provinces and Navarra from Spain as well as the three Basque provinces located in the South of France. The procedure that has been defined to achieve these goals is the "armed struggle".

Since 1968, when ETA carried out its first killing, up to last November, when it killed last, ETA has caused almost one thousand fatal casualties.

In 1975, Franco's death allowed the beginning of the longed-for democratic transition in Spain that culminated in 1978 when the Spanish people approved the Spanish Constitution by referendum. It was then when the drafting of the statutes of autonomy of the Autonomous Regions opting for self-government started. Consequently, the Basque Country has been an Autonomous Region—out of the 17 Spanish Autonomous Regions—since 1979. It has a Government that has wide-ranging powers, in some cases absolute, regarding economic, educational (special attention is paid to the Basque culture and language), security (with its own police corps), and health issues.

However, in spite of the arrival of democracy, ETA did not renounce terror.

In 1992, in order to palliate a serious internal crisis caused by the arrest of its leadership in France, ETA boosted the emergence of street-riot groups in the Basque country. Since then, these groups have been carrying out the so-called "low-intensity" terrorism.

In 1998, ETA declared an indefinite cessation of its terrorist activity, moved by its operational weakness. This "truce-tramp" lasted fourteen months that the terrorist gang used to restore its damaged structures. In order to break this "truce", ETA drove two vans loaded with 1.000 kg of explosives from the South of France in December 1999. The vans were bound for Madrid at the time of their interception. Their target was the Picasso tower, a skyscraper located in the financial centre of Madrid. In the last two years, ETA killed 38 people as a result of 120 terrorist attacks. However, the Police action both in Spain and France dismantled most of ETA's operational cells and logistic structure, respectively.

So far this year [2002], ETA has mounted four car bomb attacks in Bilbao, it has placed three packet-bombs to three Basque journalists considered by ETA as "troublesome". Just three days ago, ETA left three people wounded with a limpet bomb, leaving the Basque Socialist Youth leader seriously wounded. Likewise, in an attempt to counterbalance the weakness of its terrorist cells, it maintains alive street riots, with frequent attacks on public and private property, houses of politicians and journalists, city buses, bank branches, and so on. To a lesser extent, these actions have been spread to the French-Basque country.

Both types of attacks meet their aim at times. As a result of the intense pressure exercised by ETA, quite a number of city counsellors have resigned their posts in the last two years. In addition, many university teachers have abandoned their jobs in their respective Faculties. In the last decade, up to 200,000 citizens have left their homes in the region for other regions in Spain. A recent case in point may be revealing: last weekend a 75 year old Socialist counsellor of a small Basque village announced his resignation, because of the daily pressure on his family by radical groups. He left his home only to come to live in another part of Spain.

ETA's Terror Strategy

Terrorists have gradually broadened the range of targets by including those people that, in some way, have been involved in the defence of liberties and in the struggle against ETA's terrorism. Thus, apart from police and military forces' members, the terrorist organization has added to its list of targets members of some other groups of people considered to be "enemies"; that is, journalists, Basque autonomous police, judges, politicians of nation-wide political parties, and so on.

ETA, the clandestine structure of which is based in France, controls the whole political network that is called Movimiento de Liberación Nacional Vasco (i.e., Basque National Liberation Movement). It uses another semi-clandestine structure as the link to open organizations based mainly in Spain. These other organizations include the legal organizations.

This movement can only count on scarce backing by the Basque society: around 10%. The latest autonomic elections in the Basque Community took place in 2001, where ETA's political branch suffered a serious blow, by going from 14 down to 7 regional seats.

In spite of the effort by ETA to try to influence political life by continuing a relentless terrorist campaign, the number of terrorist attacks have declined thanks to increasing lack of social support and intensified police pressure.

ETA's Terror Logistics

The increase in percentage of the use of car bombs in its attacks is relevant; 17 cases in the year 2001 out of 56 attacks—a high proportion. Using car bombs in the attacks is defined by special characteristics that fit in ETA's current circumstances: it can only count on a scarce number of operational cells. This procedure guarantees more security for the operatives and ensures important social repercussions, resulting in social intimidation. Once the car bomb is ready in the South of France or in the Basque country, it will get exploded somewhere in Spain.

Traditionally, ETA has followed different procedures for the procurement of arms and explosives: the robbery of explosives depots from civilian companies—currently in France and before that in Spain—, manufacturing of their own and the purchase in clandestine arms and explosives trafficking markets.

As for arms, in the past ETA obtained illegal supplies in Western European countries. However, these procedures used—where occasionally ETA members travelled to acquire material—have been replaced by other more modern methods, where this terrorist group contacts European mafia-related networks dealing with arms trafficking.

Since the collapse of the communist regimes in Europe and benefiting from the confrontations in the Balkans, ETA shifted its supply networks towards these geographical areas. Like ETA, the few existing European terrorist groups get their supplies from these areas too, via some third countries. To this effect, ETA has coincided with those terrorist groups in the joint or parallel exploitation of the existent networks.

The identification and subsequent neutralisation of illegal trafficking of arms and explosives for terrorist groups are essential to hinder their activities. To this effect, the countries of origin of the material should act responsibly and fully cooperate to put an end to those activities.

ETA is funded mainly from one source: the money it collects through extortion of small and medium businessmen, charging them the so-called "revolutionary tax". At present the amounts required are between 35,000 and 400,000 euros. The annual budget the terrorist organisation needs for the maintenance of its structures is estimated at around 10 million euros.

Beyond the Spanish borders, ETA seeks links with similar groups and causes. Hence, it intends to gain the support of ideologically akin groups. It has or has had contacts with the Breton Revolutionary Army, with Corsican and Irish terrorist groups, with revolutionary groups from Latin America, etc.

In order to obtain operational and political support in Europe, ETA avails itself of the so-called "Solidarity Committees", which are small cells made up by people closely linked with ETA, and also by citizens of the country involved sometimes linked with radical left-wing, antiglobalisation, alternative and squatter movements. From the operational point of view, the joint police pressure in the Spanish and French territories has forced ETA to consider other countries where its infrastructures may be settled.

Outside Europe, some countries of Latin America are used as destination by many ETA members fleeing from police or judicial operations. These countries are considered a "third rearguard" and a temporary shelter for those who flee.

Spain's Success in Fighting the ETA

Finally, the fight against ETA's terrorism at the moment can be summarised as follows:

- ETA's operational capability is on the decrease.
- Growing police efficiency both in Spain and in France as well as bilateral co-ordination on intelligence, police and judiciary matters. This improvement has resulted from the co-operation of the French authorities and relevant bodies that has rendered excellent results in the fight against terrorism.
- Growing social rejection of violence as means to reach political goals.
- Culmination of ETA's international isolation due to the co-operation of the authorities of some Latin American countries.
- Strengthening of police, judiciary and intelligence operational bodies within the European Union such as Eurojust and Europol. As an example, in January 2001 Eurojust carried out an operation that resulted in the arrest of one of ETA's collaborators in The Netherlands.

The Spanish Presidency is fostering a greater co-ordination within the European Union on judiciary matters. Progress has been made in the common definition of the crime of terrorism and in the conditions for the arrest and handing over of terrorists among member countries (Eurowarrant) which will speed up the traditional bilateral extradition procedures.

Thank you for your attention.

GREAT
SPEECHES
IN
HISTORY

Domestic U.S. Terrorism, Then and Now

Political Violence Is the Result of Social Injustice

Emma Goldman

Anarchism is a political philosophy that advocates the elimination of formal governments. Some anarchists advocated "propaganda of the deed"—the use of violence to instigate revolt against oppressive governments. The philosophy came to America as anarchists became involved with the American labor movement in the late nineteenth century.

In 1892, a bitter labor strike erupted in the steel mills of Pennsylvania, and guards hired by the Carnegie Steel Company shot nine striking steelworkers. Two Russian-born anarchists, Alexander Berkman and Emma Goldman, decided to retaliate. On July 23, 1892, Berkman attempted, but failed, to assassinate industrialist and Carnegie executive William Clay Frick. Goldman was never charged with the crime, but Berkman was sent to prison for a term of twenty-two years.

Later, Goldman rejected terrorism, instead choosing to dedicate her life to political organizing and advocating her version of the anarchist cause. Goldman became involved in various free speech and civil liberties issues, including early feminist issues such as the subordination of women and birth control. The U.S. government labeled her "Red Emma" for her radical activities. She was jailed on several occasions and in 1908 was deprived of her U.S. citizenship. In 1917, Goldman and Berkman were tried and later imprisoned for protesting military con-

Emma Goldman, speech to the jury during her anticonscription trial, New York City, July 9, 1917.

scription for World War I. In a July 9, 1917, speech to the jury during the trial, excerpted below, Goldman defended herself against claims that she supported political violence. She explains that as a "social student," her aim is to discover the cause of such violence, which she says results from governmental violence and injustice. She rejects the notion that by endeavoring to explain the cause of political violence she is advocating it.

Ultimately, at the height of the post–World War I, anti-Communist fervor in the United States, the government deported both Goldman and Berkman to Russia in 1919. However, they left the Soviet Union after a short time, profoundly disillusioned with the new authoritarian regime of the Bolsheviks.

Gentlemen of the Jury:

As in the case of my co-defendant, Alexander Berkman, this is also the first time in my life I have ever addressed a jury. . . .

The police department failed to prove by their notes that we advised people not to register [for military conscription]. But since they had to produce something incriminating against Anarchists, they conveniently resorted to the old standby, always credited to us, "We believe in violence and we will use violence."

The Statement About Violence Is False

Assuming, gentlemen of the jury, that this sentence was really used at the meeting of May 18th [date of an Anarchist meeting], it would still fail to prove the indictment which charges conspiracy and overt acts to carry out the conspiracy. And that is all we are charged with. Not violence, not Anarchism. I will go further and say, that had the indictment been for the advocacy of violence, you gentlemen of the jury, would still have to render a verdict of "Not Guilty," since the mere belief in a thing or even the announcement that you would carry out that belief, can not possibly constitute a crime.

However, I wish to say emphatically that no such expression as "We believe in violence and we will use violence" was uttered at the meeting of May 18th, or at any other meeting. I could not have employed such a phrase, as there was no occasion for it. If for no other reason, it is because I want my lectures and speeches to be coherent and logical. The sentence credited to me is neither.

The Social Causes of Political Violence

I have read to you my position toward political violence from a lengthy essay called "The Psychology of Political Violence."

But to make that position clearer and simpler, I wish to say that I am a social student. It is my mission in life to ascertain the cause of our social evils and of our social difficulties. As a student of social wrongs it is my aim to diagnose a wrong. To simply condemn the man who has committed an act of political violence, in order to save my skin, would be as unpardonable as it would be on the part of the physician, who is called to diagnose a case, to condemn the patient because the patient has tuberculosis, cancer, or some other disease. The honest, earnest, sincere physician does not only prescribe medicine, he tries to find out the cause of the disease. And if the patient is at all capable as to means, the doctor will say to him, "Get out of this putrid air, get out of the factory, get out of the place where your lungs are being infected." He will not merely give him medicine. He will tell him the cause of the disease. And that is precisely my position in regard to acts of violence. That is what I have said on every platform. I have attempted to explain the cause and the reason for acts of political violence.

It is organized violence on top which creates individual violence at the bottom. It is the accumulated indignation against organized wrong, organized crime, organized injustice which drives the political offender to his act. To condemn him means to be blind to the causes which make him. I can no more do it, nor have I the right to, than the physician who were to condemn the patient for his disease. You and I and all of us who remain indifferent to the crimes of poverty, of war, of human degradation, are equally responsible for the act committed by the political offender. May I therefore be permitted to say, in the words of a great teacher: "He who is without sin among you, let him cast the first stone." Does that mean advocating violence? You might as well accuse Jesus of advocating prostitution, because He took the part of the prostitute, Mary Magdalene.

Black People Must Arm Themselves

Huey P. Newton

In the 1960s and 1970s, a wave of left-wing, anticapitalist terrorism swept Europe and the Americas, inspired in part by student opposition to the U.S. involvement in Vietnam. Various student groups in Europe, such as the Red Brigades in Italy and the Red Army in West Germany, participated in violent acts of terrorism against property and people with the goal of inspiring worldwide revolution in the working classes. In the United States, groups such as the Black Panthers and the Weather Underground pursued similar goals. While the Weather Underground bombed government facilities to protest the war in Vietnam, the Black Panthers promoted violent revolution, largely through armed clashes with police, as the only way to end racism in the United States.

The Black Panther Party was founded by two students in Oakland, California—Bobby G. Seale and Huey P. Newton—as a way to stop police harassment of Oakland's African American population. Members of the group conducted armed patrols of the area, leading to clashes with police. In 1967, Newton spoke at the State Capitol Building in Sacramento, California, opposing the Mulford Act, a bill aimed at regulating the Black Panthers' right to carry loaded firearms. In the speech, reprinted below, Newton argues that blacks must arm to protect themselves from a persistently oppressive, racist government. Among the group's later goals, as set forth in the Black Panther Party Platform and Program, were the arming of all blacks, the exemption of blacks from

Huey P. Newton, speech at the State Capitol Building, Sacramento, CA, May 2, 1967. Copyright © 1967 by Huey P. Newton. Reproduced by permission of Random House, Inc.

the draft, the release of all blacks from jail, and the payment of compensation to blacks for centuries of exploitation in America.

Using slogans such as "Power to the People" and gestures such as the raised fist, the party attracted thousands of followers and became the symbol of black resistance to racial oppression in the 1960s and 1970s. In 1968, two Olympic gold medalists, John Carlos and Tommy Smith, lost their medals for raising their fists in solidarity with the Black Panther movement at the Olympics.

Largely due to concerted FBI efforts to crack down on their activities, the group was largely disbanded by the 1980s.

The Black Panther Party for Self-Defense calls upon the American people in general, and Black people in particular, to take careful note of the racist California Legislature now considering legislation aimed at keeping Black people disarmed and powerless while racist police agencies throughout the country intensify the terror, brutality, murder, and repression of Black people.

At the same time that the American Government is waging a racist war of genocide in Vietnam the concentration camps in which Japanese-Americans were interned during World War II are being renovated and expanded. Since America has historically reserved its most barbaric treatment for non-White people, we are forced to conclude that these concentration camps are being prepared for Black people who are determined to gain their freedom by any means necessary. The enslavement of Black people at the very founding of this country, the genocide practiced on the American Indians and the confinement of the survivors on reservations, the savage lynching of thousands of Black men and women, the dropping of atomic bombs on Hiroshima and Nagasaki, and now the cowardly massacre in Vietnam all testify to the fact that toward people of color the racist power structure of America has but one policy: repression, genocide, terror, and the big stick.

Black people have begged, prayed, petitioned and demonstrated, among other things, to get the racist power structure of America to right the wrongs which have historically been perpetrated against Black people. All of these efforts have been answered by more repression, deceit, and hypocrisy. As the aggression of the racist American Government escalates in Vietnam, the police agencies of America escalate the repression of Black people throughout the ghettos of America. Vicious police dogs, cattle prods, and increased patrols have become familiar sights in Black communities. City Hall turns a deaf ear to the pleas of Black people for relief from this increasing terror.

The Black Panther Party for Self-Defense believes that the time has come for Black people to arm themselves against this terror before it is too late. The pending Mulford Act brings the hour of doom one step nearer. A people who have suffered so much for so long at the hands of a racist society must draw the line somewhere. We believe that the Black communities of America must rise up as one man to halt the progression of a trend that leads inevitably to their total destruction.

Fighting Terrorism Is Imperative After the Oklahoma City Bombing

Bill Clinton

In the 1980s and 1990s, domestic U.S. terrorism came largely from right-wing terrorist groups and militants—skinheads, neo-Nazis, and right-wing militia. These terrorists tend to be disorganized, with roots in white supremacist groups such as the Ku Klux Klan, and they often have racist, anti-Semitic, and antigovernment views. Many in the extreme right are influenced by a book published in 1978 called *The Turner Diaries*, by Andrew Macdonald, a fictional account of a right-wing, worldwide race war survived mostly by Aryan Americans with the goal of reordering the world according to right-wing, white supremacist, racist, and anti-Semitic views. The book is considered the treatise for what is known as anti-Zionist Occupation Government (ZOG) ideology.

In one of the most horrendous right-wing terrorist incidents, on April 19, 1995, a truck bomb exploded in front of a federal office building in Oklahoma City, Oklahoma, killing 168 and wounding more than 400. Timothy McVeigh, a right-wing conservative and gun enthusiast who had served in the U.S. Army, was convicted in June 1997 of responsibility for the bombing and executed on June 11, 2001. Although McVeigh did not belong to any extremist groups, he is reported to have been angry

Bill Clinton, radio address to the nation, April 13, 1996.

over the federal government's clashes with white separatist Randy Weaver at Ruby Ridge, Idaho, in 1992 and with David Koresh and the Branch Davidians at Waco, Texas, in 1993. He reportedly had read *The Turner Diaries* and recommended the book to others.

In response to the bombing, President Bill Clinton proposed counterterrorism legislation to provide federal law enforcement officials with better means to investigate and prevent terrorism and increased penalties for terrorism. In a speech on April 13, 1996, almost one year after the bombing, Clinton called on Congress to pass a strong antiterrorism bill. He outlined the necessary elements: explicit authority to prevent terrorist groups from raising money in the United States, authority to quickly deport foreigners who support terrorist activities, the ability to use high-tech surveillance and other investigative tools, and a provision to chemically mark the explosive materials terrorists use to build bombs. Shortly thereafter, Congress passed legislation that included some, but not all, of the president's provisions.

Most domestic terrorists in the United States today remain highly decentralized and have not undertaken dramatic terrorist acts. One other terrorist incident, however, has been credited to right-wing terrorists—a bomb exploded at the Atlanta Olympics in July 1996, killing one person and injuring many others.

T his week, on April the 19th, we mark one of America's saddest anniversaries—the first anniversary of the bombing of the Murrah Building in Oklahoma City. It is when the American spirit is at its best that we find renewal in even the most desolate of our tragedies. And that is what the people of Oklahoma City have managed somehow to do.

They have shown us that while we cannot guarantee our children a world free of madmen, we can promise them that we will always build and rebuild safe places to sustain and nurture their new lives. They have reminded us that while we can never call back the souls that were torn from us, we can prove that the forces of hatred and division are no match for the goodness in the human spirit.

The Fight Against Terrorism Must Be a Priority

Oklahoma City reminds us of something else—that we must give nothing less than everything we have in the fight against terrorism in our country and around the world, for the forces that are sparking so much of the progress we see today—lightning-fast technology, easier travel, open borders—these forces also make it easier for people with a grudge or a cause to launch a terrorist attack against innocent people.

In this new era, fighting terrorism must be a top law enforcement and national security priority for the United States. On our own and with our allies, we have put in place strong sanctions against states that sponsor terrorism. We have improved our cooperation with other nations to deter terrorists before they act, to capture them when they do, and to see to it that they are brought to justice. We've increased funding, personnel and training for our own law enforcement agencies to deal with terrorists.

But we must do even more. That is why, more than a year ago, I sent to Congress legislation that would strengthen our ability to investigate, prosecute and punish terrorist activity.

After Oklahoma City, I made it even stronger. My efforts were guided by three firm goals: First, to protect American lives without infringing on American rights. Second, to give the FBI and other law enforcement officials the tools they have asked for to do the job. And, third, to make sure terrorists are barred from this country.

Congress Must Pass the Anti-Terrorism Bill

In the wake of Oklahoma City, Congress promised to send me the bill six weeks after the tragic bombing. And yet, unbelievably, almost an entire year has passed, and Congress still has not managed to send me strong anti-terrorism legislation. There is simply no excuse for this foot-dragging. This bill should have been law a long time ago.

So I urge Congress: Make it happen. Pass anti-terrorism legislation now. In the name of the children and all the people of Oklahoma City, I say to Congress, do not let another day go by in which America does not have the tools it needs to fight terrorism. It's essential that Congress send me the right anti-terrorism legislation—legislation that finally will give law enforcement the upper hand.

When I met with leaders of the congressional majority shortly after the bombing, they assured me that Congress would give the American people strong anti-terrorism legislation. They haven't. While the Senate passed a solid bill, the House absolutely gutted it. Under pressure from the Washington gun lobby, House Republicans took that bill apart, piece by piece. Well, now, it's time they put it back together. America cannot afford to settle for a fake anti-terrorism bill. We need the real thing. And on my watch, I'm determined to get it.

Elements Necessary for a Strong Anti-Terrorism Bill

This is what real anti-terrorism should have: First, we need explicit authority to prevent terrorist groups like Hamas from raising money in the United States for their dirty deeds. Second, we need authority to deport quickly foreigners who abuse our hospitality by supporting terrorist activities away from or within our shores.

Second, we need to give law enforcement officials the ability to use high-tech surveillance and other investigative tools to keep up with stealthy, fast-moving terrorists.

And we need a provision to mark chemically the explosive materials terrorists use to build their deadly bombs. If we know where the explosives come from, we have an edge in tracking down the criminals who use them. These taggants work. In fact, when they were being tested just a few years ago, they helped us to catch a man who had killed someone with a car bomb. Law enforcement officials believe that of the more than 13,000 bombing crimes in the last five years, as many as 30 percent could have been solved faster with taggants.

Yet, the Republicans in Congress continue to oppose this common-sense initiative. Why? Because the Washington gun lobby told them to. One Republican congressman had another reason—an unbelievable one. He actually told his own committee chairman, "I trust Hamas more than my own government." Well, I don't. And I don't think most Americans or most members of Congress in either party do.

I urge Congress to change course. Put the national interest before the special interests. Give law enforcement the ability to trace these explosives using bombs that kill Americans.

We know acts of terror are no match for the human spirit. In the last year, the people of Oklahoma City have proved this. We know we can heal from terrorism. But now we must do even more to stop it before it happens. A strong anti-terrorism bill will help us to do just that. And that's why it must be the law of the land.

CHAPTER

FOUR

Islamic Fundamentalist Terrorism and September 11, 2001

America Declares War on Terror

George W. Bush

Much contemporary international terrorism is perpetrated by adherents to a militant strain of fundamentalist
Islam. In recent years, the United States has found itself
the object of fundamentalist Islamic terrorist strikes at
home and abroad, including a 1993 bombing at the
World Trade Center in New York City, which caused 6
deaths and numerous injuries, a 1998 bomb attack on the
U.S. embassies in Kenya and Tanzania, which killed 224
(12 of them Americans), and a 2000 attack in Yemen on
the USS *Cole*, killing 17 sailors and wounding 30.

On September 11, 2001, Islamic fundamentalist terrorism invaded America with a vengeance. Two commercial airliners piloted by hijackers were flown into the twin
towers of the World Trade Center in New York City. The
buildings collapsed, killing thousands of civilians and injuring many more. Another plane hit the Pentagon, and a
fourth crashed on its way toward the U.S. Capitol. On
September 20, 2001, U.S. president George W. Bush, in
an address to Congress and the nation, excerpted here,
claimed that al-Qaeda, a fundamentalist Islamic terrorist
group based in Afghanistan and led by Osama bin Laden,
was responsible for the terrorist acts. Bush declared war
on terror and demanded that the Afghanistan regime, the
Taliban, turn over al-Qaeda leaders and terrorists and
close all terrorist bases in the country.

The speech marked the beginning of a worldwide cooperative effort to find and destroy al-Qaeda and similar
terrorist groups. It also signaled a U.S. intention to con-

George W. Bush, speech before a Joint Session of Congress, Washington, DC, September 20, 2001.

duct a military assault on countries, such as Afghanistan, that harbor terrorists. When the Taliban in Afghanistan refused U.S. demands to turn over al-Qaeda operatives, the United States on October 7, 2001, attacked that country, and over the next few months ousted the Taliban regime and destroyed al-Qaeda bases there. The United States has also targeted al-Qaeda terrorists elsewhere and has disrupted, but not destroyed, the group's ability to conduct large-scale terrorist strikes.

Americans have known the casualties of war, but not at the center of a great city on a peaceful morning. Americans have known surprise attacks, but never before on thousands of civilians. All of this was brought upon us in a single day, and night fell on a different world, a world where freedom itself is under attack. Americans have many questions. They are asking, who attacked our country? The evidence we have gathered all points to a collection of loosely affiliated terrorist organizations known as al Qaeda. They are the same murderers indicted for bombing American embassies in Tanzania and Kenya and responsible for bombing the USS *Cole*. Al Qaeda is to terror what the mafia is to crime. But its goal is not making money; its goal is remaking the world and imposing its radical beliefs on people everywhere.

Al Qaeda's Organization and Vision

The terrorists practice a fringe form of Islamic extremism that has been rejected by Muslim scholars and the vast majority of Muslim clerics, a fringe movement that perverts the peaceful teachings of Islam. The terrorists' directive commands them to kill Christians and Jews, to kill all Americans, and make no distinction among military and civilians, including women and children. This group and its leader, a person named Osama bin Laden, are linked to many other organizations in different countries, including the Egyptian Islamic Jihad and the Islamic Movement of Uzbekistan. There are thousands of these terrorists in more than 60 countries. They are recruited from their own nations and neighborhoods and brought to camps in places like Afghanistan, where they are trained in the tactics of terror. They are sent back to their homes or sent to hide in countries around the world to plot evil and destruction. The leadership of al Qaeda has great influence in Afghanistan and supports the Taliban regime in controlling most of that country.

In Afghanistan, we see al Qaeda's vision for the world. Afghanistan's people have been brutalized, many are starving and many have fled. Women are not allowed to attend school. You can be jailed for owning a television. Religion can be practiced only as their leaders dictate. A man can be jailed in Afghanistan if his beard is not long enough. The United States respects the people of Afghanistan, after all, we are currently its largest source of humanitarian aid, but we condemn the Taliban regime. It is not only repressing its own people, it is threatening people everywhere by sponsoring, sheltering and supplying terrorists. By aiding and abetting murder, the Taliban regime is committing murder. And the United States of America makes the following demands on the Taliban. Deliver to the United States authorities all the leaders of al Qaeda who hide in your land. Release all foreign nationals, including American citizens, you have unjustly imprisoned. Protect foreign journalists, diplomats and aid workers in your country. Close immediately and permanently every terrorist training camp in Afghanistan, and hand over every terrorist and every person in their support structure to appropriate authorities. Give the United States full access to terrorist training camps, so we can make sure they are no longer operating. These demands are not open to negotiation or discussion.

The Taliban must act, and act immediately. They will hand over the terrorists, or they will share in their fate. I also want to speak directly to Muslims throughout the world. We respect your faith. It's practiced freely by many millions of Americans and by millions more in countries that America counts as friends. Its teachings are good and peaceful, and those who commit evil in the name of Allah blaspheme the name of Allah. The terrorists are traitors to their own faith, trying, in effect, to hijack Islam itself. The enemy of America is not our many Muslim friends, and it is not our many Arab friends. Our enemy is a radical network of terrorists and every government that supports them. Our war on terror begins with al Qaeda, but it does not end there. It will not end until every terrorist group of global reach has been found, stopped and defeated.

Why Do They Hate Us?

Americans are asking, why do they hate us? They hate a democratically elected government. Their leaders are self-appointed. They hate our freedoms. Our freedom of religion, our freedom of speech, our freedom to vote and assemble and disagree with each other. They want to overthrow existing governments in many Muslim countries, such as Egypt, Saudi Arabia and Jordan. They want to drive Israel out of the Middle East. They want to drive Christians and Jews out of vast regions of Asia and Africa. These terrorists kill not merely to end lives, but to disrupt and end a way of life.

With every atrocity, they hope that America grows fearful, retreating from the world and forsaking our friends. They stand against us, because we stand in their way. We are not deceived by their pretenses to piety. We have seen their kind before. They are the heirs of all the murderous ideologies of the 20th century. By sacrificing human life to serve their radical visions, by abandoning every value except the will to power, they follow in the path of fascism, Nazism and totalitarianism. And they will follow that path all the way, to where it ends in history's unmarked grave of discarded lies.

A Lengthy Campaign to Fight Terror

Americans are asking how will we fight and win this war? We will direct every resource at our command, every means of diplomacy, every tool of intelligence, every instrument of law enforcement, every financial influence and every necessary weapon of war, to the disruption and to the defeat of the global terror network. This war will not be like the war against Iraq a decade ago, with a decisive liberation of territory and a swift conclusion. It will not look like the air war above Kosovo two years ago, where no ground troops were used and not a single American was lost in combat.

Our response involves far more than instant retaliation and isolated strikes. Americans should not expect one battle, but a lengthy campaign, unlike any other we have ever seen. It may include dramatic strikes, visible on TV, and covert operations, secret even in success. We will starve terrorists of funding, turn them one against another, drive them from place to place, until there is no refuge or no rest. And we will pursue nations that provide aid or safe haven to terrorism. Every nation, in every region, now has a decision to make. Either you are with us, or you are with the terrorists. From this day forward, any nation that continues to harbor or support terrorism will be regarded by the United States as a hostile regime.

Our nation has been put on notice. We are not immune from attack. We will take defensive measures against terrorism to protect Americans. Dozens of federal departments and agencies, as well as state and local governments, have responsibilities affecting homeland security. These efforts must be coordinated at the highest level. I announce the creation of a cabinet-level position reporting directly to me—the Office of Homeland Security. And I also announce that a distinguished American has been chosen to lead this effort, to strengthen American security. A military veteran, an effective governor, a true patriot, a trusted friend—Pennsylvania's Tom Ridge. He will lead, oversee and coordinate a comprehensive national strategy to safeguard our country against terrorism and respond to any attacks that may come. These measures are essential. But the only way to defeat terrorism as a threat to our way of life is to stop it, eliminate it and destroy it where it grows. Many will be involved in this effort, from FBI agents to intelligence operatives to the reservists we have called to active duty. All deserve our thanks, and all have our prayers. And a few miles from the damaged Pentagon, I have a message for our military: Be ready.

Other Nations Will Help Us

I've called the armed forces to alert, and there is a reason. The hour is coming when America will act, and you will make us proud. This is not, however, just America's fight. And what is at stake is not just America's freedom. This is the world's fight. This is civilization's fight. This is the fight of all who believe in progress and pluralism, tolerance and freedom. We ask every nation to join us. We will ask, and we will need, the help of police forces, intelligence services and banking systems around the world. The United States is grateful that many nations and many international organizations have already responded—with sympathy and with support. Nations from Latin America, to Asia, to Africa, to Europe, to the Islamic world. Perhaps the NATO [North Atlantic Treaty Organization] Charter reflects best the attitude of the world: An attack on one is an attack on all. The civilized world is rallying to America's side. They understand that if this terror goes unpunished, their own cities, their own citizens may be next. Terror, unanswered, can not only bring down buildings, it can threaten the stability of legitimate governments. And we're not going to allow it. Americans are asking, what is expected of us? I ask you to live your lives and hug your children. I know many citizens have fears tonight, and I ask you to be calm and resolute, even in the face of a continuing threat. I ask you to uphold the values of America, and remember why so many have come here. We are in a fight for our principles, and our first responsibility is to live by them. No one should be singled out for unfair treatment or unkind words because of their ethnic background or religious faith. . . .

Our Mission Is Clear

After all that has just passed—all the lives taken, and all the possibilities and hopes that died with them—it is natural to wonder if America's future is one of fear. Some speak of an age of terror. I know there are struggles ahead, and dangers to face. But this country will define our times, not be defined by them. As long as the United States of America is determined and strong, this will not be an age of terror; this will be an age of liberty, here and across the world. Great harm has been done to us. We have suffered great loss. And in our grief and anger we have found our mission and our moment.

Freedom and fear are at war. The advance of human freedom—the great achievement of our time and the great hope of every time—now depends on us. Our nation—this generation—will lift a dark threat of violence from our people and our future. We will rally the world to this cause by our efforts, by our courage. We will not tire, we will not falter, and we will not fail. It is my hope that in the months and years ahead, life will return almost to normal. We'll go back to our lives and routines, and that is good. Even grief recedes with time and grace. But our resolve must not pass. Each of us will remember what happened that day and to whom it happened. We'll remember the moment the news came—where we were and what we were doing. Some will remember an image of a fire or a story of rescue. Some will carry memories of a face and a voice gone forever. And I will carry this. It is the police shield of a man named George Howard who died at the World Trade Center trying to save others. It was given to me by his mom, Arlene, as a proud memorial to her son. This is my reminder of lives that ended and a task that does not end.

I will not forget this wound to our country or those who inflicted it. I will not yield; I will not rest; I will not relent in waging this struggle for freedom and security for the American people. The course of this conflict is not known, yet its outcome is certain. Freedom and fear, justice and cruelty, have always been at war, and we know that God is not neutral between them. Fellow citizens, we'll meet violence with patient justice—assured of the rightness of our cause and confident of the victories to come. In all that lies before us, may God grant us wisdom, and may He watch over the United States of America.

Al-Qaeda Thanks God for the September 11 Attacks on America

Osama bin Laden

Shortly after the September 11, 2001, terrorist attacks in New York and Washington, D.C., U.S. president George W. Bush demanded that Afghanistan's Taliban government turn over al-Qaeda terrorists to the United States. The Taliban failed to comply with this demand. As a result, on October 7, 2001, the United States and Britain attacked the Taliban regime and al-Qaeda bases in Afghanistan.

Shortly after the U.S. military began its assault in Afghanistan, on October 7, 2001, the Arabic television news network Al-Jazeera broadcast a videotape showing Osama bin Laden, the leader of al-Qaeda, making the following speech in which he praises God for the September 11 attacks and swears America will not be secure until its armies leave the "land of Muhammad." Many viewed the tape as proof of al-Qaeda's responsibility for the killings.

Thereafter, Al-Jazeera broadcast two other bin Laden videotapes, on November 3, 2001, and on December 26, 2001, each showing a progressively more unhealthy-looking bin Laden. Another videotape was released by the Pentagon on December 13, 2001, in which bin Laden is shown laughing with colleagues while discussing the World Trade Center terrorist attacks and stating that al-Qaeda had calculated the number of casualties in ad-

Osama bin Laden, videotaped speech aired on Al-Jazeera, October 7, 2001.

vance. This tape appeared to confirm al-Qaeda's responsibility for the September 11 attack beyond any question. Despite concerted efforts by U.S. military and intelligence forces to find bin Laden, dead or alive, his whereabouts remain unknown. The United States, however, defeated the Taliban regime in Afghanistan and destroyed al-Qaeda's bases there, and America continues its efforts to find and destroy al-Qaeda terrorists elsewhere around the world.

I bear witness that there is no God but Allah and that Muhammad is his messenger.

There is America, hit by God in one of its softest spots. Its greatest buildings were destroyed, thank God for that. There is America, full of fear from its north to its south, from its west to its east. Thank God for that.

What America is tasting now is something insignificant compared to what we have tasted for scores of years. Our nation (the Islamic world) has been tasting this humiliation and this degradation for more than 80 years. Its sons are killed, its blood is shed, its sanctuaries are attacked, and no one hears and no one heeds.

When God blessed one of the groups of Islam, vanguards of Islam, they destroyed America. I pray to God to elevate their status and bless them.

Arab Lives Lost

Millions of innocent children are being killed as I speak. They are being killed in Iraq without committing any sins, and we don't hear condemnation or a fatwa (religious decree) from the rulers. In these days, Israeli tanks infest Palestine—in Jenin, Ramallah, Rafah, Beit Jalla, and other places in the land of Islam, and we don't hear anyone raising his voice or moving a limb.

When the sword comes down (on America), after 80 years, hypocrisy rears its ugly head. They deplore and they lament for those killers, who have abused the blood, honor

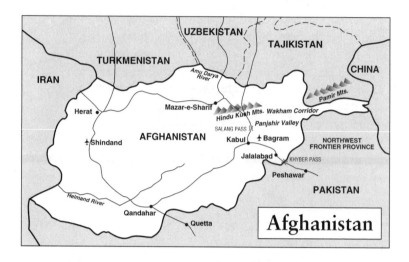

and sanctuaries of Muslims. The least that can be said about those people is that they are debauched. They have followed injustice. They supported the butcher over the victim, the oppressor over the innocent child. May God show them His wrath and give them what they deserve.

America Fights Islam in the Name of Terrorism

I say that the situation is clear and obvious. After this event, after the senior officials have spoken in America, starting with the head of infidels worldwide, Bush, and those with him. They have come out in force with their men and have turned even the countries that belong to Islam to this treachery, and they want to wag their tail at God, to fight Islam, to suppress people in the name of terrorism.

America's Hypocrisy

When people at the ends of the earth, Japan, were killed by their hundreds of thousands, young and old, it was not considered a war crime, it is something that has justification. Millions of children in Iraq is something that has justification. But when they lose dozens of people in Nairobi and Dar es Salaam (capitals of Kenya and Tanzania, where U.S. embassies were bombed in 1998), Iraq was struck and Afghanistan was struck.

Hypocrisy stood in force behind the head of infidels worldwide, behind the cowards of this age, America and those who are with it.

These events have divided the whole world into two sides. The side of believers and the side of infidels, may God keep you away from them. Every Muslim has to rush to make his religion victorious. The winds of faith have come. The winds of change have come to eradicate oppression from the island of Muhammad, peace be upon him.

No Security for America

To America, I say only a few words to it and its people. I swear by God, who has elevated the skies without pillars, neither America nor the people who live in it will dream of security before we live it in Palestine, and not before all the infidel armies leave the land of Muhammad, peace be upon him.

God is great, may pride be with Islam. May peace and God's mercy be upon you.

America and Israel Are the True Terrorists

Sayyed Hasan Nassrallah

President Bush, in his speeches after September 11, 2001, claimed that an "underworld" of Islamic terrorist groups, including not only al-Qaeda but also groups such as Hamas, Hezbollah, Islamic Jihad, and Jaish-i-Mohammed, existed in the Middle East. Some of these groups, such as Hamas and Hezbollah, seek Palestinian independence and the end to Israeli occupation of Palestine.

Hamas, for example, was founded in 1987 as a radical alternative to the Palestine Liberation Organization (PLO) headed by Yasser Arafat. The group, unlike the PLO, seeks to establish an Islamic state in Palestine and insists on the destruction of Israel. In the 1990s Hamas stepped up its terrorist activities as the PLO became more political, and Arafat's efforts to limit Hamas terrorism have largely failed.

Another Islamic terrorist group, Hezbollah, which means "party of God," is closely connected with Iran's Shiite Islamic revolution. The group began in Lebanon during the Lebanese Civil War in the 1970s and is heavily dependent on Iranian financial and military assistance. After Israel invaded Lebanon in 1982, Hezbollah attacked Israel and has since become involved on the side of the Palestinians in the Israeli-Palestinian conflict. Like Hamas, Hezbollah calls for the ouster of Israel from Palestine.

The political leader of Hezbollah is Sayyed Hasan Nassrallah, secretary general of the group since 1992. In

Sayyed Hasan Nassrallah, speech marking the first anniversary of the second Palestinian Intifada, September 28, 2001.

a speech given on September 28, 2001, marking the first anniversary of the second Palestinian Intifada (uprising) against Israel, Nassrallah argues that the Palestinian resistance to Israel's occupation of Palestinian land is not terrorism. In the speech, he rejects America's definition of "terrorism" and claims that Israel's occupation of Palestine, which is supported by the United States, is the worst kind of terrorism. This position represents the views of not only Hezbollah but also other Palestinian resistance groups in the area, such as Hamas.

We meet again in this place that has witnessed many occasions marking dates of resistance and martyrdom. However, the marking of this anniversary is one of the means that shows our support of and solidarity with the Palestinian people and its steadfastness and determination to regain its dignity and holy shrines.

After one year the Intifada [uprising] still exists in our minds and priorities and remains the major concern of Arabs and Moslems. From this place we salute all those who have shown solidarity and held demonstrations anywhere in the world.

Events in the Struggle of Palestinian Resistance

Today I would like to remind you of some past events that took place in September. I want to remind you of the massacre of September 13th, 1993 that was carried out against our people who took to the streets to denounce the Oslo agreement in which two thirds of the Palestinian Land was forfeited with the other third remaining in a state of ambiguity. At that time several criminals fired at the chests and heads of the demonstrators that led to the killing of nine persons and the wounding of 50 others.

The conspirators wanted to create a battle between the Lebanese Army and the Resistance and its people and revenge to Israel. However, we remember those days and feel proud that our people were perceptive and sensible enough to not involve themselves in any internal conflict, keeping as their priority the fight against Israel.

In these days we also remember the heroic confrontation in (Insaria) on [September 5, 1997], which led to the killing of a unit of Israel's elite forces. The Insaria confrontation not only constituted a hard blow to the morale of the Israeli occupation forces but it was primarily a tough strike to the Israeli intelligence and remained a mystery on how the Islamic Resistance could discover the Israeli commando force in advance. The Insaria mystery will remain so and the time hasn't come yet to be revealed.

We want also to remember the confrontation in the Jabal al-Rafi that took place a few days after the Insaria confrontation in which the blood of the Resistance men mixed with the blood of the Lebanese Army soldiers.

Disruption of Israeli Normalization

In the first anniversary of the start of the Intifada the Palestinians turned their struggle into a real resistance that sees victory coming soon. The Intifada has sacrificed 725 martyrs, 30 thousand injured and 1500 current detainees. In addition there are the former detainees to consider as well as constant suffering and hardship.

The Intifada could shake the bases of the so-called (normalization) and direct a massive blow to the Israeli plan, which aims to normalize in order to be accepted and enter the Arab world with its aim of hegemony.

The Intifada in Palestine shook the bases of the Israeli plan. America and some Arab countries have worked on the normalization project. However the Intifada came and defeated Israeli plans with stones and bullets. The Palestinian people could put down the normalization current and unveil the reality of the Zionist's racism.

One year after the Oslo agreement, more than one million Jews settled in Palestine and there is no distinction between a Jewish militant and Jewish civilian, they are all occupiers who have come to seize Palestinian land.

The Palestinian Intifada and resistance shook the doctrine of the Promised Land and many Zionists started to question if they were in the right place. The Intifada complemented what the resistance has started in Lebanon. Executing military operations in the 1948 occupied land has more influence and effect in making the victory closer. These operations gave a tough blow to the opportunities of investment and led to the decline of immigration to Palestine and increase of the opposite immigration. All these achievements will make the victory very close.

Effects of September 11, 2001

Recent events in the U.S. have temporarily pushed away the Palestinian Intifada from the center stage of international and Arab attention. I believe that these events have a deep link regarding the likely reasons or the expected results with the current conflict in the region.

Since September 11, the Israeli enemy rushed to accuse the Islamic movements in Lebanon and Palestine and concentrated on some names like, Hizbollah, Hamas and Islamic Jihad. This happened at a time when all of America was in confusion. If the Israelis had such information why they have waited until now to reveal it, why they didn't give it to the U.S. in advance?

On the other hand America rushed to accuse the Arabs and Muslims as being those behind the attacks, placing them in the circle of blame, increasing the wave of hatred against Arabs and Muslims all over the U.S., Canada and Australia. Shortly afterwards, the American administration declared a war on terrorism and spoke of forming an international coalition against terrorism.

In light of recent developments I would like to mention the following: The Arabs, Muslims and their governments, parties and clerics denounce the killing of innocent people anywhere in the world whether it is Hiroshima, Nagasaki, Deir Yassin, Sabra and Shatila, Qana or New York.

American Hypocrisy About Terrorism

It is distressing to see that the entire world is expected to take part in the denouncing hysteria only because the events occurred in America and those killed are American.

When Arabs or Muslims are killed as happened in Sabra, Shatila and Qana then this is an entirely different issue. The American administration didn't denounce those or other massacres. In addition, it prevented the international community from denouncing such actions and used its veto in the U.N. Security Council to do so.

America rejects the idea of trying war criminals like Arial Sharon, the Israeli Prime minister as well as [Israeli leaders Shimon] Peres, [Ehud] Barak and others. It also refuses to label them as terrorists despite evidence and documentation proving that they have committed massacres and that they are the ones who killed 725 Palestinians while the world looked on and turned a deaf ear. The evidence exists, but the U.S. doesn't call this terrorism, at the same time it wants to punish all Afghanistan because the prime suspect is Osama Bin Ladin and he only resides in that country.

Millions of Afghans escaped their country to areas where no shelter and food because of fear of American strikes and because the American administration suspects Bin Ladin whereas the Israeli leaders and the Israeli Army stand accused by irrefutable evidence, yet must not be brought to justice. It is a shame that in the view of the American Administration, Israel is considered the oasis of "Democracy" and "Civilization" in the Middle East and that it is the one America depends on to fight "terrorism". This is American Justice.

America Practices Terrorism by Supporting Israel

The America that wants an international coalition itself practices terrorism through support of Israel, the most dangerous entity in the world.

I want to emphasize that America is not honest in fighting terrorism and the proof is its support to Israel. It also is not qualified to lead an international coalition for the reasons I mentioned earlier. America will continue its support of some terrorist groups in the world while at the same time creating an image of a generic Muslim enemy.

After the collapse of the Soviet Union they said Islam is

the new enemy but when they found that more than one billion would be their enemies and that that would work counter to U.S. interests, they fell back and divided Islam into two groups, moderates and extremists. American arrogance and superiority implies that it should create an enemy and now it is terrorism. Bush has declared his war against terrorism and declared the coalition of good and Justice in the face of terrorism and Osama Bin Ladin. But what is next?

America's Goal Is Domination

The U.S. has set up its goals and it is not serious. It is only a pretext to increase its domination in the world and a pretext to have military presence in Afghanistan and mid Asia very close to the Qezzween Sea. America wants its bases to spread anywhere in the world and it is prohibited to any to oppose but whoever opposes becomes accused of harboring terrorism. It must be very clear to every Arab and Muslim and any honored man in this world that [it] is prohibited to offer any sort of support to America in its aggression against the people of Afghanistan.

We reject the arrogant rhetoric of Bush in the U.S. Congress and we consider it an enormous insult to all governments and peoples of the world. We consider any aggression against Afghanistan to be an aggression against innocent and oppressed people and it will face denunciation from our side.

Call for Opposition to America's War

We call on all to set aside fear and not to be subject to American dictation. What brings hope is that many countries in the world did not answer the American call. Many countries have spoken out, some calling for reason and wisdom, others saying we have to define terrorism and some want the United Nations to lead and the Security Council to lead the campaign against terrorism. I respect those who have raised their concerns. Bush imagined that the world would obediently prostrate itself before him, surrendering to his leadership.

I thank the leaders of Lebanon, Syria and Iran and all governments of [the] Arab and Islamic world who refused to label Lebanese and Palestinian resistance as terrorist groups.

I want to advise some Arab and Muslim leaderships, specifically some enthusiastic Islamic movements, not to be dragged into what the U.S. has called a crusade war. If this was the intent of Bush we shouldn't be dragged into that. No Muslim should consider that this is a war of Christianity against Islam. It is a tragedy if we think that way.

The Zionist desire is to see a world war between Christians and Muslims. The majority of Muslims and Christians reject terrorism and have honored positions in fighting Israel and Zionism. Some have sacrificed themselves for the legitimate cause of Lebanon, Palestine and Syria and the Arab and Islamic world. No one should be dragged into a war of this kind.

Anyone in this world who destroys a church in retaliation for setting a mosque on fire is acting in the Zionists interest. The declared war against Arab and Muslims has only something to do with the materialistic, capitalist and arrogant mentality and has nothing to do with Jesus Christ or with Christianity or with Christians. We have to be wise enough, I am deeply concerned that some extremist Arab and Islamists who are closed-minded may infiltrate our body and we may be dragged into reaction. We don't need to be enticed to any state of reactionary anger or to fall for this trap. At this time we need the highest degree of wisdom and reason.

Hizbollah Will Continue Palestinian Resistance

We are determined to pursue the line of Resistance until our land is liberated and detainees in Israeli prisons are freed. We will continue our support of the Palestinian people in their Intifada with money, weapons, media coverage and public presence. I want to reiterate and say to our Palestinian people that if we wanted to swap the Lebanese detainees for the four Israeli soldiers that we have we were able to [do] that. However, we insist in all negotiation rounds with the German mediators that the Palestinian detainees must be part of the swap operation. We continue to discuss with the mediators the number of the detainees in a way that preserves the dignity of the struggling people of Palestine.

We will continue our support of the Palestinian Resistance and we are ready for direct military interference from Lebanese territory when we feel that the Palestinian Resistance is in urgent need for that support. Our position after the events of September 11th remains unchanged from the position we held prior to September 11th. What goals were pursued before that date will continue to be pursued after that date. September 11th may have changed America or the world but does not change our position and will not affect our right to liberate our land and to free our detainees.

All of us must be armed with faith in God and self-confidence to face future dangerous periods as we have in the past.

CHAPTER
FIVE

Terrorism and Weapons of Mass Destruction

The New Terrorists and the Proliferation of Weapons of Mass Destruction

Thomas Graham Jr.

In the past, terrorists often had political or social goals, such as seeking independence or fomenting revolution. Past terrorist actions typically involved assassinations or bombings that targeted police or military and usually did not injure large numbers of persons. Even before the September 11, 2001, attack on the World Trade Center, however, there was concern about a new breed of terrorists who seek indiscriminate killing of civilians rather than specific targets, with no particular political or other demands. Attacks such as the first World Trade Center bombing by al-Qaeda in 1993 and the subway sarin gas attack by the Aum Shinrikyo cult in Japan in 1995 illustrated this phenomenon.

In a speech on September 19, 1996, reprinted here, Ambassador Thomas Graham Jr., the special representative of the president for arms control, nonproliferation, and disarmament, outlined these new concerns about international terrorism and weapons of mass destruction. He explained that the collapse of the Soviet Union and its police state have made it more likely that nuclear materials can be stolen and sold to terrorists. Furthermore, rogue states that support terrorists, such as Iran and Iraq, have increased their efforts to acquire weapons of mass destruction.

Thomas Graham Jr., speech before a Law Enforcement and Intelligence Conference, Washington, DC, September 19, 1996.

The September 11 attack brought these concerns to the attention of the entire world, although there appears to be disagreement about what strategy should be pursued to defend against such terrorism. The U.S. Bush administration has formulated a new national security policy that emphasizes the need for taking preemptive action against terrorists and terrorist states that might threaten the United States or seek possession of weapons of mass destruction that could threaten the world. Because this approach is a departure from past American and international policies that favored a defensive rather than offensive posture, the "Bush doctrine" has proven controversial.

I'm sure we all remember the day three and a half years ago when a group of terrorists exploded a van filled with explosives under the World Trade Center in New York and the realization it brought that American soil was not immune to the plague of terrorism. Following in the wake of that stunning realization was a chilling question asked by many: what if, instead of a mixture of fertilizer and fuel, the van had held a crude nuclear device containing a few kilograms of plutonium? The World Trade Center and everything for blocks in every direction would have been completely destroyed and the death toll would have been in the hundreds of thousands. Radiation would have hampered rescue efforts and much of New York City would have been contaminated by fallout.

Similar scenarios have been used in movies and books over the years, but only recently have we begun to understand how real the threat of a terrorist attack using weapons of mass destruction (WMD)—nuclear, biological or chemical (NBC) weapons—has become. I would like to share with you three reasons why I feel the threat of a terrorist group unleashing a nuclear device or other weapon of mass destruction upon the world has grown. The first involves the collapse of the Soviet Union, the second concerns the increased efforts by rogue states to acquire weapons of mass destruction, and the third reason is a change in the nature of terrorism itself.

When the Soviet Union disintegrated in the early 1990's, it was not readily apparent that this historic transformation would pose such a potentially dangerous situation. However, the change from a police state, where crime was virtually non-existent and movement was tightly controlled, to an environment where organized gangs are a major societal force and some military officers engage in corruption has made the once unthinkable suddenly possible: the so-called "loose nukes" scenario wherein nuclear materials are stolen and sold to a pariah state, terrorist group, or organized crime. The end of the Cold War left Russia with a huge surplus of nuclear weapons and material—approximately 1,200 metric tons of highly-enriched uranium and 200 metric tons of plutonium, translatable into scores of thousands of potential nuclear weapons—which can be expected to grow as Russia continues to dismantle nuclear weapons. Whereas this material was once kept under tight control, the reorganization of its armed forces and its struggling economy have left Russia's nuclear stockpile less well guarded than it should be. As a recent report by the General Accounting Office (GAO) described the situation:

> Social and economic changes in the newly independent states have increased the threat of theft and diversion of nuclear material, and with the breakdown of Soviet-era MPC&A [Material, Protection, Control and Accounting] systems, the newly independent states may not be as able to counter the increased threat. Nuclear facilities rely on antiquated accounting systems that cannot quickly detect and localize nuclear material losses. Many facilities lack modern equipment that can detect unauthorized attempts to remove nuclear material from facilities.

GAO personnel who visited Russia in 1995 found that some facilities did not have a comprehensive inventory of their nuclear materials on hand and, incredibly, the visitors were in one instance able to gain access to fissile material without even showing identification to the lone unarmed security guard in the building. During the investigation in 1993 of a theft of enriched uranium used as fuel for naval propulsion reactors, a Russian military prosecutor was reported as saying that at the time of the theft, potatoes were guarded better than nuclear fuel. The danger of nuclear materials leaking out of the former Soviet Union has received much publicity over the last year, but this is not an over-hyped issue of interest only to academics and those of us in the arms control community. Preventing the theft of nuclear materials from facilities in the former Soviet Union is one of the most important problems facing the world today, and it is crucial that we keep uranium and plutonium from falling into the wrong hands.

Efforts by Rogue States to Acquire WMD

While the collapse of the Soviet Union created new fears about nuclear materials leaking out to terrorists or criminals, the efforts of rogue states such as Iran and Iraq to acquire weapons of mass destruction is an old danger that has become more threatening in recent years. Few rational people fear that these states will develop a strategic missile force capable of threatening the United States in the foreseeable future, but their history of supporting and sponsoring terrorist activities makes the possibility of their possession of weapons of mass destruction troubling. It is easy to imagine Iraq or Libya, frustrated by their inability to defeat the United States militarily, deciding to smuggle a nuclear, chemical or biological weapon into the United States or near our armed forces abroad as a means of seeking revenge. Press reports of Iran's attempts to buy fissile material on the black market and their continuing efforts to develop nuclear technology are reason for alarm. We know now how close Iraq was to building a nuclear weapon just prior to the Gulf War, and Saddam Hussein continues to hide information concerning the Iraqi chemical, biological and nuclear weapon programs from UN inspectors. In Libya, construction has ceased for the time being on what we think is a massive chemical weapons plant at Tarhunah, but who knows how long this halt will last? These states, and several others, who have time and again shown that they operate outside the circle of civilized nations by supporting terrorism, must be prevented from acquiring weapons of mass destruction at all costs.

In addition to the two factors I have just described, the possibility of a terrorist group using a nuclear, chemical, or biological weapon has increased simply because terrorism itself seems to have changed. Terrorists no longer single-mindedly seek publicity, as they did in the 1970's and 80's. Many of today's terrorists remain anonymous and attempt to kill as many people as possible, with seemingly no rhyme or reason. Walter Laqeuer, writing in the most recent issue of Foreign Affairs, points out that, "the trend now seems to be away from attacking specific targets . . . and toward more indiscriminate killing." For example, the Aum Shin Rikyo cult in Japan, who last year unleashed sarin gas on unsuspecting subway passengers, was trying to bring about the deaths of thousands of innocent civilians and made no attempt to claim responsibility or publicity for their actions. The perpetrators of the Oklahoma City bombing had no compunctions about killing hundreds of innocents merely because they happened to work in a federal building. The modern breed of terrorist seeks only to kill. If such terrorists gain access to a nuclear device, or chemical or biological weapons, they will likely seek to use them.

Chemical and Biological Weapons Easy to Acquire

Frighteningly, it is not difficult to gain access to these weapons. The complexities involved in obtaining and handling fissile material put nuclear devices beyond the capability of all but the most advanced terrorist groups, but chemical and biological weapons are surprisingly easy to manufacture or buy. Law enforcement officials investigating the Aum Shin Rikyo compound after the subway attack found that this previously unknown group had a stockpile of chemical warfare agents and was attempting to develop biological weapons as well.

Investigators also discovered that the group had in fact actually staged several previous small scale chemical attacks that went unnoticed. Most frightening of all, it does not take a group as large or well-funded as Aum Shin Rikyo to gain access to such weapons. In March 1995, a man with ties to the white supremacist group Aryan Nation purchased an organism that causes bubonic plague from a medical supply company in Rockville, Maryland. Fortunately, because of our domestic implementing law for the Biological Weapons Treaty, the company also notified the authorities and the vials were recovered unopened. Also in 1995, authorities apprehended and convicted two members of a Minnesota militia organization for the possession of ricin, a poisonous protein which they had produced themselves. The Oklahoma City tragedy proved to us that terror is as likely to come from individuals or small groups of people born and raised in this country as it is from a foreign band of religious extremists or political radicals.

Barriers to Proliferation of Nuclear Weapons

To sum up, then, both the supply of weapons of mass destruction and the terrorist demand for them have increased over the last decade. Although the threat that terrorists will use these weapons is greater now than it has ever been, we are not helpless—we can take steps to make such an occurrence less likely. Some important measures have already been taken, and include efforts to improve the safety and security of nuclear material in the former Soviet Union, international agreements aimed at eliminating weapons of mass destruction or preventing rogue states from acquiring them, and improving our ability to deal with these threats if and when they occur.

The Cooperative Threat Reduction program (CTR), created in 1991 through legislation sponsored by Senators Sam Nunn and Richard Lugar, has already made progress in improving the safety of Russian nuclear materials. The United States has set aside roughly $1 billion for CTR projects. The program faced some difficult obstacles in its first few years of existence in the form of lingering Cold War suspicions, but after reaching agreement with the Russian Ministry of Atomic Energy on access to Russian facilities in January 1995, the speed of implementation has improved dramatically and the program has been expanded to several new sites.

The international community has also worked together to prevent terrorists or rogue states from acquiring weapons of mass destruction. Last year's indefinite extension of the Nuclear Nonproliferation Treaty (NPT) was a significant step forward in fighting the proliferation of nuclear weapons to rogue states. With 182 countries party to the now permanent NPT, it is clear the international community has taken a stand against the further spread of nuclear weapons. Before the NPT entered into force in 1970, the acquisition of nuclear weapons capability had often been a point of national pride. The NPT has made it tantamount to a violation of international law and has added immeasurably to the security of the United States and of the entire world. The NPT is the cornerstone of the nuclear nonproliferation regime, which also includes international safeguards on nuclear materials and multilateral nuclear export control guidelines.

The Comprehensive Test Ban Treaty (CTBT) will represent another barrier against proliferation by making it more difficult for new states to develop nuclear weapons and by preventing nuclear weapons states from developing new ones. A CTBT is in the best interest of the United States because it will prevent a new arms race and keep other states from building nuclear arsenals, and it is in the interest of every other nation in the world for these same reasons. Much like the NPT, the CTBT is a "common sense" agreement.

International Efforts

While the fight against nuclear proliferation is extremely important, chemical or biological weapons are increasingly more likely to be used by a terrorist group. Fortunately, the international community has also taken steps to make it more difficult for terrorists to acquire such weapons.

The "Australia Group," an informal forum of 30 states, including the United States, is chaired by Australia, and has as its goal to discourage and impede chemical and biological weapon proliferation by harmonizing national export controls on precursor chemicals, pathogens, and dual-use production equipment, sharing information on proliferation developments, and seeking other ways to curb the use of chemical and biological weapons.

The Biological Weapons Convention (BWC) entered into

force in 1975, and has 138 parties who have pledged not to in any circumstances develop, produce, stockpile or otherwise acquire or retain microbial or other biological agents, or toxins whatever their origin or method of production, of types and in quantities that have no justification for prophylactic, protective or other peaceful purposes. Unlike other regimes, the BWC contains no provisions for on-site compliance activity, a source of increasing criticism in recent years. In an effort to strengthen the BWC, the United States is currently actively participating in an effort to draft a legally binding protocol that will enhance openness and transparency through, among other things, on-site activities.

The Chemical Weapons Convention of 1993 (CWC) will ban the stockpile, transfer, and production of chemical weapons and will require parties to submit to intrusive on-site inspections. Due to its comprehensive verification regime, this treaty, which was drafted in consultation with representatives from our chemical industry, is a landmark in the struggle against the proliferation of weapons of mass destruction. The Convention will make it tougher for rogue states like Iraq to acquire chemical weapons and will increase the safety of our citizens at home as well as our troops in the field.

I deeply regret that last week, the Senate had to postpone final debate on the CWC. This delays the day we protect America's soldiers and citizens by outlawing all chemical weapons—poison gas, including highly toxic nerve gas and related chemicals. But rather than risk losing the treaty, it made sense to postpone debate while both elected branches and both parties seek to reach agreement on ways to secure the universal support the Convention deserves.

U.S. Defenses Against Terrorist Attacks

Fortunately, in the United States, we have a robust law enforcement and intelligence capability to combat terrorist attacks. Intelligence and law enforcement officials prevented attacks on the United Nations and the Holland Tunnel in New York and also prevented an attempt to bomb American passenger planes over the Pacific Ocean. Those responsible for the World Trade Center bombing were convicted and suspects in the Oklahoma City and Unabomber cases have been taken into custody. These successes send an important message to would-be terrorists: that the United States is ready, willing and able to fight them. However, despite these achievements, we must work even harder and make sure our law enforcement and intelligence communities continue to improve their capability to defeat terrorism in whatever form it takes. In this regard, I am glad to note that under the leadership of Senators Nunn and Lugar, the Senate recently agreed to legislation mandating $150 million to strengthen our ability to detect terrorist attacks before they happen and to improve our capability to deal with such attacks if they occur.

I must note that I find it somewhat ironic that while a very expensive national missile defense program has become a highly publicized political issue, less attention is paid to fighting the proliferation of weapons of mass destruction, despite overwhelming evidence that a nuclear or chemical attack is more likely to come in the form of a suitcase or parked van than a ballistic missile. I would like to stress the importance of combating the proliferation of weapons of mass destruction and the need to continue to improve our capability to prevent, detect, and deal with the threat of weapon of mass destruction terrorism before we are forced to do so by an unimaginable tragedy. The attacks that occurred in New York, Oklahoma City and Tokyo were horrible, but they have given us some powerful lessons. I fervently hope it does not take yet another terrible incident to move us to action.

It was Edmund Burke who said the only thing necessary for the triumph of evil is for good men to do nothing. If we do not redouble our efforts to prevent terrorists from acquiring and using weapons of mass destruction, then I am afraid it is only a matter of time before we will be witness to another triumph of evil.

The United States Should Expect Future Terrorist Attacks

George J. Tenet

September 11, 2001, awakened the United States to the threat from terrorist attacks against Americans and from terror-supporting nations acquiring weapons of mass destruction. Several months after the September 11 attack, on February 6, 2002, George J. Tenet, director of the U.S. Central Intelligence Agency, testified before the Senate Select Committee on Intelligence about the current terrorist threat against the United States. In his testimony, excerpted here, Tenet declares that al-Qaeda remains a threat, that other terrorist groups such as Hezbollah are dedicated to attacking Americans, and that states such as Iran and Iraq continue to support terrorist groups that target the United States. The United States, Tenet said, is particularly concerned that these terrorist groups or regimes will acquire weapons of mass destruction. He explains that chemical and biological weapons are difficult to monitor because they can also be used for nonmilitary purposes and because they are easily concealed within commercial facilities. Nuclear weapons, together with new missile technologies, also pose a significant threat because of the difficulty of detecting material and technology transfers to terrorists or terrorist regimes.

Tenet's testimony paints a picture of frightening possibilities, requiring long-term, continued U.S. vigilance

George J. Tenet, testimony before the Senate Select Committee on Intelligence, Washington, DC, February 6, 2002.

against terrorist threats. Although no incidents of the scale of September 11 have occurred since Tenet's speech, several smaller terrorist actions against the United States and Western targets have been attributed to terrorists. In October 2002, for example, terrorists who may be affiliated with al-Qaeda struck a tourist nightclub in Bali, killing two hundred. In a separate attack, a U.S. diplomat was killed in Jordan.

Mr. Chairman, I appear before you this year under circumstances that are extraordinary and historic for reasons I need not recount. Never before has the subject of this annual threat briefing had more immediate resonance. Never before have the dangers been more clear or more present.

September 11 brought together and brought home—literally—several vital threats to the United States and its interests that we have long been aware of. It is the convergence of these threats that I want to emphasize with you today: the connection between terrorists and other enemies of this country, the weapons of mass destruction they seek to use against us, and the social, economic, and political tensions across the world that they exploit in mobilizing their followers. September 11 demonstrated the dangers that arise when these threats converge—and it reminds us that we overlook at our own peril the impact of crises in remote parts of the world.

America Remains a Nation at War

This convergence of threats has created the world I will present to you today—a world in which dangers exist not only in those places where we have most often focused our attention, but also in other areas that demand it.

In places like Somalia, where the absence of a national government has created an environment in which groups sympathetic to al-Qaida have offered terrorists an operational base and potential haven.

In places like Indonesia, where political instability, sepa-

ratist and ethnic tensions, and protracted violence are ham-
pering economic recovery and fueling Islamic extremism.

In places like Colombia, where leftist insurgents who
make much of their money from drug trafficking are escalating their assault on the government—further undermining
economic prospects and fueling a cycle of violence.

And finally, Mr. Chairman, in places like Connecticut,
where the death of a 94-year-old woman in her own home of
anthrax poisoning can arouse our worst fears about what
our enemies might try to do to us.

These threats demand our utmost response. The United
States has clearly demonstrated since September 11 that it is
up to the challenge. But make no mistake: despite the battles
we have won in Afghanistan, we remain a nation at war.

Al-Qaida Remains a Threat

Last year I told you that Osama bin Ladin and the al-Qaida
network were the most immediate and serious threat this
country faced. This remains true today despite the progress
we have made in Afghanistan and in disrupting the network
elsewhere. We assess that al-Qaida and other terrorist groups
will continue to plan to attack this country and its interests
abroad. Their modus operandi is to have multiple attack
plans in the works simultaneously, and to have al-Qaida cells
in place to conduct them.

We know that terrorists have considered attacks in the
U.S. against high-profile government or private facilities, famous landmarks, and U.S. infrastructure nodes such as air-
ports, bridges, harbors, and dams. High profile events such
as the Olympics or last weekend's Super Bowl also fit the terrorists' interest in striking another blow within the United
States that would command worldwide media attention.

Al-Qaida also has plans to strike against U.S. and allied
targets in Europe, the Middle East, Africa, and Southeast
Asia. American diplomatic and military installations are at
high risk—especially in East Africa, Israel, Saudi Arabia, and
Turkey.

Operations against U.S. targets could be launched by al-
Qaida cells already in place in major cities in Europe and the

Middle East. Al-Qaida can also exploit its presence or connections to other groups in such countries as Somalia, Yemen, Indonesia, and the Philippines.

Threat of Unconventional Weapons and Attacks

Although the September 11 attacks suggest that al-Qaida and other terrorists will continue to use conventional weapons, one of our highest concerns is their stated readiness to attempt unconventional attacks against us. As early as 1998, bin Ladin publicly declared that acquiring unconventional weapons was "a religious duty."

Terrorist groups worldwide have ready access to information on chemical, biological, and even nuclear weapons via the Internet, and we know that al-Qaida was working to acquire some of the most dangerous chemical agents and toxins. Documents recovered from al-Qaida facilities in Afghanistan show that bin Ladin was pursuing a sophisticated biological weapons research program.

We also believe that bin Ladin was seeking to acquire or develop a nuclear device. Al-Qaida may be pursuing a radioactive dispersal device—what some call a "dirty bomb."

Alternatively, al-Qaida or other terrorist groups might also try to launch conventional attacks against the chemical or nuclear industrial infrastructure of the United States to cause widespread toxic or radiological damage.

We are also alert to the possibility of cyber warfare attack by terrorists. September 11 demonstrated our dependence on critical infrastructure systems that rely on electronic and computer networks. Attacks of this nature will become an increasingly viable option for terrorists as they and other foreign adversaries become more familiar with these targets, and the technologies required to attack them.

Threat from Other Terrorist Groups

The terrorist threat goes well beyond al-Qaida. The situation in the Middle East continues to fuel terrorism and anti-U.S. sentiment worldwide. Groups like the Palestine Islamic Jihad

(PIJ) and Hamas have escalated their violence against Israel, and the intifada has rejuvenated once-dormant groups like the Popular Front for the Liberation of Palestine. If these groups feel that U.S. actions are threatening their existence, they may begin targeting Americans directly—as Hizballah's terrorist wing already does.

The terrorist threat also goes beyond Islamic extremists and the Muslim world. The Revolutionary Armed Forces of Colombia (FARC) poses a serious threat to U.S. interests in Latin America because it associates us with the government it is fighting against.

The same is true in Turkey, where the Revolutionary People's Liberation Party/Front has publicly criticized the United States and our operations in Afghanistan.

We are also watching states like Iran and Iraq that continue to support terrorist groups.

Iran continues to provide support—including arms transfers—to Palestinian rejectionist groups and Hizballah. Tehran has also failed to move decisively against al-Qaida members who have relocated to Iran from Afghanistan.

Iraq has a long history of supporting terrorists, including giving sanctuary to Abu Nidal.

The war on terrorism has dealt severe blows to al-Qaida and its leadership. The group has been denied its safehaven and strategic command center in Afghanistan. Drawing on both our own assets and increased cooperation from allies around the world, we are uncovering terrorists' plans and breaking up their cells. These efforts have yielded the arrest of nearly 1,000 al-Qaida operatives in over 60 countries, and have disrupted terrorist operations and potential terrorist attacks.

Mr. Chairman, bin Ladin did not believe that we would invade his sanctuary. He saw the United States as soft, impatient, unprepared, and fearful of a long, bloody war of attrition. He did not count on the fact that we had lined up allies that could help us overcome barriers of terrain and culture. He did not know about the collection and operational initiatives that would allow us to strike—with great accuracy—at the heart of the Taliban and al-Qaida. He underestimated our capabilities, our readiness, and our resolve.

That said, I must repeat that al-Qaida has not yet been destroyed. It and other like-minded groups remain willing and able to strike us. Al-Qaida leaders still at large are working to reconstitute the organization and to resume its terrorist operations. We must eradicate these organizations by denying them their sources of financing and eliminating their ability to hijack charitable organizations for their terrorist purposes. We must be prepared for a long war, and we must not falter.

The Conditions That Create Terrorism

Mr. Chairman, we must also look beyond the immediate danger of terrorist attacks to the conditions that allow terrorism to take root around the world. These conditions are no less threatening to U.S. national security than terrorism itself. The problems that terrorists exploit—poverty, alienation, and ethnic tensions—will grow more acute over the next decade. This will especially be the case in those parts of the world that have served as the most fertile recruiting grounds for Islamic extremist groups.

We have already seen—in Afghanistan and elsewhere—that domestic unrest and conflict in weak states is one of the factors that create an environment conducive to terrorism.

More importantly, demographic trends tell us that the world's poorest and most politically unstable regions—which include parts of the Middle East and Sub-Saharan Africa—will have the largest youth populations in the world over the next two decades and beyond. Most of these countries will lack the economic institutions or resources to effectively integrate these youth into society.

The Role of Islam in Terrorism

All of these challenges come together in parts of the Muslim world, and let me give you just one example. One of the places where they converge that has the greatest long-term impact on any society is its educational system. Primary and secondary education in parts of the Muslim world is often dominated by an interpretation of Islam that teaches intolerance and hatred. The graduates of these schools—"madrasas"—provide the foot soldiers for many of the Islamic militant groups that operate throughout the Muslim world.

Let me underscore what the President has affirmed: Islam itself is neither an enemy nor a threat to the United States. But the increasing anger toward the West—and toward governments friendly to us—among Islamic extremists and their sympathizers clearly is a threat to us. We have seen—and continue to see—these dynamics play out across the Muslim world. Let me briefly address their manifestation in several key countries.

The Campaign in Afghanistan

Our campaign in Afghanistan has made great progress, but the road ahead is fraught with challenges. The Afghan people, with international assistance, are working to overcome a traditionally weak central government, a devastated infrastructure, a grave humanitarian crisis, and ethnic divisions that deepened over the last 20 years of conflict. The next few months will be an especially fragile period.

Interim authority chief Hamid Karzai will have to play a delicate balancing game domestically. Remaining al Qaida fighters in the eastern provinces, and ongoing power struggles among Pashtun leaders there underscore the volatility of tribal and personal relations that Karzai must navigate.

Taliban elements still at large and remaining pockets of Arab fighters could also threaten the security of those involved in reconstruction and humanitarian operations. Some leaders in the new political order may allow the continuation of opium cultivation to secure advantages against their rivals for power.

The Political Shift in Pakistan

Let me move next to Pakistan. September 11 and the U.S. response to it were the most profound external events for Pakistan since the Soviet invasion of Afghanistan in 1979, and the U.S. response to that. The Musharraf government's alignment with the U.S.—and its abandonment of nearly a decade of support for the Taliban—represent a fundamental political shift with inherent political risks because of the militant Islamic and anti-American sentiments that exist within Pakistan.

President Musharraf's intention to establish a moderate, tolerant Islamic state—as outlined in his 12 January speech—is being welcomed by most Pakistanis, but he will still have to confront major vested interests. The speech is energizing debate across the Muslim world about which vision of Islam is the right one for the future of the Islamic community.

Musharaff established a clear and forceful distinction between a narrow, intolerant, and conflict-ridden vision of the past and an inclusive, tolerant, and peace-oriented vision of the future.

The speech also addressed the jihad issue by citing the distinction the Prophet Muhammad made between the "smaller jihad" involving violence and the "greater jihad" that focuses on eliminating poverty and helping the needy.

Although September 11 highlighted the challenges that India–Pakistan relations pose for U.S. policy, the attack on the Indian Parliament on December 13 was even more destabilizing—resulting as it did in new calls for military action against Pakistan, and subsequent mobilization on both sides. The chance of war between these two nuclear-armed states is higher than at any point since 1971. If India were to conduct large scale offensive operations into Pakistani Kashmir, Pakistan might retaliate with strikes of its own in the belief that its nuclear deterrent would limit the scope of an Indian counterattack.

Both India and Pakistan are publicly downplaying the risks of nuclear conflict in the current crisis. We are deeply concerned, however, that a conventional war—once begun—could escalate into a nuclear confrontation.

Iraqi President Saddam Hussein Remains a Threat

Let me turn now to Iraq. Saddam has responded to our progress in Afghanistan with a political and diplomatic charm offensive to make it appear that Baghdad is becoming more flexible on U.N. sanctions and inspections issues. Last month he sent Deputy Prime Minister Tariq Aziz to Moscow and Beijing to profess Iraq's new openness to meet its U.N. obligations and to seek their support.

Baghdad's international isolation is also decreasing as support for the sanctions regime erodes among other states in the region. Saddam has carefully cultivated neighboring states, drawing them into economically dependent relationships in hopes of further undermining their support for the sanctions. The profits he gains from these relationships provide him the means to reward key supporters and, more importantly, to fund his pursuit of WMD. His calculus is never about bettering or helping the Iraqi people.

Let me be clear: Saddam remains a threat. He is determined to thwart U.N. sanctions, press ahead with weapons of mass destruction, and resurrect the military force he had before the Gulf war. Today, he maintains his vise grip on the levers of power through a pervasive intelligence and security apparatus, and even his reduced military force—which is less than half its pre-war size—remains capable of defeating more poorly armed internal opposition groups and threatening Iraq's neighbors.

As I said earlier, we continue to watch Iraq's involvement in terrorist activities. Baghdad has a long history of supporting terrorism, altering its targets to reflect changing priorities and goals. It has also had contacts with al-Qaida. Their ties may be limited by divergent ideologies, but the two sides' mutual antipathy toward the United States and the Saudi royal family suggests that tactical cooperation between them is possible—even though Saddam is well aware that such activity would carry serious consequences.

Iran's Support for Terrorism

In Iran, we are concerned that the reform movement may be losing its momentum. For almost five years, President Khatami and his reformist supporters have been stymied by Supreme Leader Khamenei and the hardliners.

The hardliners have systematically used the unelected institutions they control—the security forces, the judiciary, and the Guardian's Council—to block reforms that challenge their entrenched interests. They have closed newspapers, forced members of Khatami's cabinet from office, and arrested those who have dared to speak out against their tactics.

Discontent with the current domestic situation is widespread and cuts across the social spectrum. Complaints focus on the lack of pluralism and government accountability, social restrictions, and poor economic performance. Frustrations are growing as the populace sees elected institutions such as the Majles and the Presidency unable to break the hardliners' hold on power.

The hardline regime appears secure for now because security forces have easily contained dissenters and arrested potential opposition leaders. No one has emerged to rally reformers into a forceful movement for change, and the Iranian public appears to prefer gradual reform to another revolution. But the equilibrium is fragile and could be upset by a miscalculation by either the reformers or the hardline clerics.

For all of this, reform is not dead. We must remember that the people of Iran have demonstrated in four national elections since 1997 that they want change and have grown disillusioned with the promises of the revolution. Social, intellectual, and political developments are proceeding, civil institutions are growing, and new newspapers open as others are closed.

The initial signs of Tehran's cooperation and common cause with us in Afghanistan are being eclipsed by Iranian efforts to undermine U.S. influence there. While Iran's officials express a shared interest in a stable government in Afghanistan, its security forces appear bent on countering the U.S. presence. This seeming contradiction in behavior reflects deep-seated suspicions among Tehran's clerics that the United States is committed to encircling and overthrowing them—a fear that could quickly erupt in attacks against our interests.

We have seen little sign of a reduction in Iran's support for terrorism in the past year. Its participation in the attempt to transfer arms to the Palestinian Authority via the Karine-A probably was intended to escalate the violence of the intifada and strengthen the position of Palestinian elements that prefer armed conflict with Israel.

The current conflict between Israel and the Palestinians

has been raging for almost a year and a half, and it continues to deteriorate. The violence has hardened the public's positions on both sides and increased the longstanding animosity between Israeli Prime Minister Sharon and Palestinian leader Arafat. Although many Israelis and Palestinians say they believe that ultimately the conflict can only be resolved through negotiations, the absence of any meaningful security cooperation between Israel and the Palestinian Authority—and the escalating and uncontrolled activities of the Palestine Islamic Jihad and Hamas—make any progress extremely difficult.

We are concerned that this environment creates opportunities for any number of players—most notably Iran—to take steps that will result in further escalation of violence by radical Palestinian groups.

At the same time, the continued violence threatens to weaken the political center in the Arab world, and increases the challenge for our Arab allies to balance their support for us against the demands of their publics.

The Proliferation of Weapons of Mass Destruction

I turn now to the subject of proliferation. I would like to start by drawing your attention to several disturbing trends in this important area. WMD [weapons of mass destruction] programs are becoming more advanced and effective as they mature, and as countries of concern become more aggressive in pursuing them. This is exacerbated by the diffusion of technology over time—which enables proliferators to draw on the experience of others and to develop more advanced weapons more quickly than they could otherwise. Proliferators are also becoming more self-sufficient. And they are taking advantage of the dual-use nature of WMD—and missile-related technologies to establish advanced production capabilities and to conduct WMD—and missile-related research under the guise of legitimate commercial or scientific activity.

Let me address in turn the primary categories of WMD proliferation, starting with chemical and biological weapons. The CBW threat continues to grow for a variety of reasons, and to present us with monitoring challenges. The dual-use nature of many CW and BW agents complicates our assessment of offensive programs. Many CW and BW production capabilities are hidden in plants that are virtually indistinguishable from genuine commercial facilities. And the technology behind CW and BW agents is spreading. We assess there is a significant risk within the next few years that we could confront an adversary—either terrorists or a rogue state—who possesses them.

On the nuclear side, we are concerned about the possibility of significant nuclear technology transfers going undetected. This reinforces our need to more closely examine emerging nuclear programs for sudden leaps in capability. Factors working against us include the difficulty of monitoring and controlling technology transfers, the emergence of new suppliers to covert nuclear weapons programs, and the possibility of illicitly acquiring fissile material. All of these can shorten timelines and increase the chances of proliferation surprise.

On the missile side, the proliferation of ICBM and cruise missile designs and technology has raised the threat to the U.S. from WMD delivery systems to a critical threshold. As outlined in our recent National Intelligence Estimate on the subject, most Intelligence Community agencies project that by 2015 the U.S. most likely will face ICBM threats from North Korea and Iran, and possibly from Iraq. This is in addition to the longstanding missile forces of Russia and China. Short—and medium—range ballistic missiles pose a significant threat now.

Several countries of concern are also increasingly interested in acquiring a land-attack cruise missile (LACM) capability. By the end of the decade, LACMs could pose a serious threat to not only our deployed forces, but possibly even the U.S. mainland.

Countries That Develop and Supply Nuclear Technology

Russian entities continue to provide other countries with technology and expertise applicable to CW, BW, nuclear, and ballistic and cruise missile projects. Russia appears to be the first choice of proliferant states seeking the most advanced technology and training. These sales are a major source of funds for Russian commercial and defense industries and military R&D.

Russia continues to supply significant assistance on nearly all aspects of Tehran's nuclear program. It is also providing Iran assistance on long-range ballistic missile programs.

Chinese firms remain key suppliers of missile-related technologies to Pakistan, Iran, and several other countries. This is in spite of Beijing's November 2000 missile pledge not to assist in any way countries seeking to develop nuclear-capable ballistic missiles. Most of China's efforts involve solid-propellant ballistic missile development for countries that are largely dependent on Chinese expertise and materials, but it has also sold cruise missiles to countries of concern such as Iran.

We are closely watching Beijing's compliance with its bilateral commitment in 1996 not to assist unsafeguarded nuclear facilities, and its pledge in 1997 not to provide any new nuclear cooperation to Iran.

Chinese firms have in the past supplied dual-use CW-related production equipment and technology to Iran. We remain concerned that they may try to circumvent the CW-related export controls that Beijing has promulgated since acceding to the CWC and the nuclear Nonproliferation Treaty.

North Korea continues to export complete ballistic missiles and production capabilities along with related raw materials, components, and expertise. Profits from these sales help Pyongyang to support its missile—and probably other WMD—development programs, and in turn generate new products to offer to its customers—primarily Iran, Libya, Syria, and Egypt. North Korea continues to comply with the terms of the Agreed Framework that are directly related to the freeze on its reactor program, but Pyongyang has warned that it is prepared to walk away from the agreement if it concluded that the United States was not living up to its end of the deal.

Iraq continues to build and expand an infrastructure capable of producing WMD. Baghdad is expanding its civilian chemical industry in ways that could be diverted quickly to CW production. We believe it also maintains an active and capable BW program; Iraq told UNSCOM it had worked with several BW agents. We believe Baghdad continues to pursue ballistic missile capabilities that exceed the restrictions imposed by U.N. resolutions. With substantial foreign assistance, it could flight-test a longer-range ballistic missile within the next five years. It may also have retained the capability to deliver BW or CW agents using modified aircraft or other unmanned aerial vehicles. We believe Saddam never abandoned his nuclear weapons program. Iraq retains a significant number of nuclear scientists, program documentation, and probably some dual-use manufacturing infrastructure that could support a reinvigorated nuclear weapons program. Baghdad's access to foreign expertise could support a rejuvenated program, but our major near-term concern is the possibility that Saddam might gain access to fissile material.

Iran remains a serious concern because of its across-the-board pursuit of WMD and missile capabilities. Tehran may be able to indigenously produce enough fissile material for a nuclear weapon by late this decade. Obtaining material from outside could cut years from this estimate. Iran may also flight-test an ICBM later this decade, using either Russian or North Korean assistance. Having already deployed several types of UAVs—including some in an attack role—Iran may seek to develop or otherwise acquire more sophisticated LACMs. It also continues to pursue dual-use equipment and expertise that could help to expand its BW arsenal, and to maintain a large CW stockpile.

Both India and Pakistan are working on the doctrine and tactics for more advanced nuclear weapons, producing fissile material, and increasing their nuclear stockpiles. We have continuing concerns that both sides may not be done with nuclear testing. Nor can we rule out the possibility that either country could deploy their most advanced nuclear weapons without additional testing. Both countries also continue development of long-range nuclear-capable ballistic missiles, and plan to field cruise missiles with a land-attack capability.

As I have mentioned in years past, we face several unique challenges in trying to detect WMD acquisition by proliferant states and non-state actors. Their use of denial and deception tactics, and their access to a tremendous amount of information in open sources about WMD production, complicate our efforts. So does their exploitation of space. The unique spaceborne advantage that the U.S. has enjoyed over the past few decades is eroding as more countries—including China and India—field increasingly sophisticated reconnaissance satellites. Today there are three commercial satellites collecting high-resolution imagery, much of it openly marketed. Foreign military, intelligence, and terrorist organizations are exploiting this—along with commercially available navigation and communications services—to enhance the planning and conduct of their operations.

Let me mention here another danger that is closely related to proliferation: the changing character of warfare itself. As demonstrated by September 11, we increasingly are facing real or potential adversaries whose main goal is to cause the United States pain and suffering, rather than to achieve traditional military objectives. Their inability to match U.S. military power is driving some to invest in "asymmetric" niche capabilities. We must remain alert to indications that our adversaries are pursuing such capabilities against us. . . .

Mr. Chairman, I want to end my presentation by reaffirming what the President has said on many occasions regarding the threats we face from terrorists and other adversaries. We cannot—and will not—relax our guard against these enemies. If we did so, the terrorists would have won. And that will not happen. The terrorists, rather, should stand warned that we will not falter in our efforts, and in our commitment, until the threat they pose to us has been eliminated.

Saddam Hussein Is a Grave and Gathering Threat to Peace

George W. Bush

In 1990, Iraq invaded its neighboring country of Kuwait. Iraqi president Saddam Hussein's refusal to withdraw as demanded by the United Nations (UN) resulted in a military strike on Iraq by a coalition of forces headed by the United States. The UN also imposed economic sanctions that continue to the present day and conducted weapons inspections until 1998, when inspectors were withdrawn because of Hussein's lack of cooperation. The inspectors found and destroyed much of the Iraqi weapons arsenal, including chemical, biological, and nuclear technology, but many fear Iraq has renewed its weapons development programs since 1998.

After the September 11, 2001, terrorist attacks in New York and Washington, D.C., the United States began to view states such as Iraq, which had a history of supporting terrorists and a thirst for weapons of mass destruction, as a higher threat than it had previously believed them to be. In January 2002, in his State of the Union address, President George W. Bush claimed that Iraq, Iran, and North Korea make up an "axis of evil" because they sponsor terrorism and seek to develop weapons of mass destruction. In later speeches, Bush threatened a preemptive, unilateral military action against Iraq to overthrow Hussein, claiming Iraq is an imminent threat due to

George W. Bush, speech to the United Nations, New York, September 12, 2002.

the suspension of UN weapons inspections there and Saddam Hussein's known efforts to continue development of chemical, biological, and nuclear weaponry. Bush was criticized at home and abroad for not seeking UN cooperation in his efforts to contain Iraq.

On September 12, 2002, President Bush brought his case against Iraq to the UN in a speech (excerpted below) that laid out Iraq's violation of numerous UN resolutions concerning disarmament and related issues. Bush asked the UN to take action to prevent the Hussein regime from developing nuclear, chemical, and biological weapons. The speech galvanized world opinion against Iraq, leading to efforts to develop a new UN resolution to force the return of weapons inspectors to Iraq for unconditional monitoring of its weapons programs. Hussein quickly bowed to international pressure, offering to permit inspectors to return under terms negotiated earlier with the UN. Bush, however, sought stronger action against Iraq, including authorization for military action, and the United States began negotiating with other members of the UN Security Council to develop a resolution that would effectively monitor Iraqi weapons disarmament and allow quick action in the event of Iraqi noncompliance. On November 8, the UN passed such a resolution. Thereafter, UN weapons inspectors returned to Iraq. After Iraq failed, in the U.S. view, to disarm and cooperate fully with the inspectors, the United States began to push for military action against Iraq.

Mr. Secretary-General, Mr. President, distinguished ladies and gentlemen: We meet one year and one day after a terrorist attack brought grief to my country, and to the citizens of many countries. Yesterday, we remembered the innocent lives taken that terrible morning. Today, we turn to the urgent duty of protecting other lives, without illusion and without fear.

We have accomplished much in the last year—in Afghanistan and beyond. We have much yet to do—in Afghanistan and beyond. Many nations represented here have joined in the fight against global terror—and the people of the United States are grateful.

The United Nations was born in the hope that survived a world war—the hope of a world moving toward justice, escaping old patterns of conflict and fear. The founding members resolved that the peace of the world must never again be destroyed by the will and wickedness of any man. We created a United Nations Security Council, so that—unlike the League of Nations—our deliberations would be more than talk, and our resolutions would be more than wishes. After generations of deceitful dictators, broken treaties and squandered lives, we dedicate ourselves to standards of human dignity shared by all, and to a system of security defended by all. . . .

Our common security is challenged by regional conflicts—ethnic and religious strife that is ancient but not inevitable. In the Middle East, there can be no peace for either side without freedom for both sides. America stands committed to an independent and democratic Palestine, living beside Israel in peace and security. Like all other people, Palestinians deserve a government that serves their interests and listens to their voices. My nation will continue to encourage all parties to step up to their responsibilities as we seek a just and comprehensive settlement to the conflict.

Above all, our principles and our security are challenged today by outlaw groups and regimes that accept no law of morality and have no limit to their violent ambitions. In the attacks on America a year ago, we saw the destructive intentions of our enemies. This threat hides within many nations, including my own. In cells and camps, terrorists are plotting further destruction and building new bases for their war against civilization. And our greatest fear is that terrorists will find a shortcut to their mad ambitions when an outlaw regime supplies them with the technologies to kill on a massive scale.

Saddam Hussein Has Failed to Comply with U.N. Resolutions

In one place—in one regime—we find all these dangers, in their most lethal and aggressive forms . . . exactly the kind of aggressive threat the United Nations was born to confront.

Twelve years ago, Iraq invaded Kuwait without provocation. And the regime's forces were poised to continue their march to seize other countries and their resources. Had Saddam Hussein been appeased instead of stopped, he would have endangered the peace and stability of the world. Yet this aggression was stopped—by the might of coalition forces, and the will of the United Nations.

To suspend hostilities and to spare himself, Iraq's dictator accepted a series of commitments. The terms were clear: to him, and to all. And he agreed to prove he is complying with every one of those obligations.

He has proven instead only his contempt for the United Nations, and for all his pledges. By breaking every pledge—by his deceptions, and by his cruelties—Saddam Hussein has made the case against himself.

In 1991, Security Council Resolution 688 demanded that the Iraqi regime cease at once the repression of its own people, including the systematic repression of minorities—which, the Council said, "threaten(ed) international peace and security in the region."

This demand goes ignored. Last year, the U.N. Commission on Human Rights found that Iraq continues to commit "extremely grave violations" of human rights and that the regime's repression is "all pervasive." Tens of thousands of political opponents and ordinary citizens have been subjected to arbitrary arrest and imprisonment, summary execution, and torture by beating, burning, electric shock, starvation, mutilation, and rape. Wives are tortured in front of their husbands; children in the presence of their parents—all of these horrors concealed from the world by the apparatus of a totalitarian state.

In 1991, the U.N. Security Council, through Resolutions 686 and 687, demanded that Iraq return all prisoners from Kuwait and other lands. Iraq's regime agreed. It broke its promise. Last year the Secretary-General's high-level coordinator of this issue reported that Kuwaiti, Saudi, Indian, Syrian, Lebanese, Iranian, Egyptian, Bahraini, and Omani nationals remain unaccounted for—more than 600 people. One American pilot is among them.

In 1991, the U.N. Security Council, through Resolution 687, demanded that Iraq renounce all involvement with terrorism, and permit no terrorist organizations to operate in Iraq. Iraq's regime agreed. It broke its promise. In violation of Security Council Resolution 1373, Iraq continues to shelter and support terrorist organizations that direct violence against Iran, Israel, and Western governments. Iraqi dissidents abroad are targeted for murder. In 1993, Iraq attempted to assassinate the Emir of Kuwait and a former American President. Iraq's government openly praised the attacks of September 11th. And al-Qaida terrorists escaped from Afghanistan are known to be in Iraq.

In 1991, the Iraqi regime agreed to destroy and stop developing all weapons of mass destruction and long-range missiles, and to prove to the world it has done so by complying with rigorous inspections. Iraq has broken every aspect of this fundamental pledge.

Hussein's Failure to Disarm

From 1991 to 1995, the Iraqi regime said it had no biological weapons. After a senior official in its weapons program defected and exposed this lie, the regime admitted to producing tens of thousands of liters of anthrax and other deadly biological agents for use with Scud warheads, aerial bombs, and aircraft spray tanks. U.N. inspectors believe Iraq has produced two to four times the amount of biological agents it declared, and has failed to account for more than three metric tons of material that could be used to produce biological weapons. Right now, Iraq is expanding and improving facilities that were used for the production of biological weapons.

United Nations inspections also reveal that Iraq likely maintains stockpiles of VX, mustard, and other chemical agents, and that the regime is rebuilding and expanding facilities capable of producing chemical weapons.

And in 1995—after four years of deception—Iraq finally admitted it had a crash nuclear weapons program prior to the Gulf War. We know now, were it not for that war, the regime in Iraq would likely have possessed a nuclear weapon no later than 1993.

Today, Iraq continues to withhold important information about its nuclear program—weapons design, procurement logs, experiment data, an accounting of nuclear materials, and documentation of foreign assistance. Iraq employs capable nuclear scientists and technicians. It retains physical infrastructure needed to build a nuclear weapon. Iraq has made several attempts to buy high-strength aluminum tubes used to enrich uranium for a nuclear weapon. Should Iraq acquire fissile material, it would be able to build a nuclear weapon within a year. And Iraq's state-controlled media has reported numerous meetings between Saddam Hussein and his nuclear scientists, leaving little doubt about his continued appetite for these weapons.

Iraq also possesses a force of Scud-type missiles with ranges beyond the 150 kilometers permitted by the U.N. Work at testing and production facilities shows that Iraq is building more long-range missiles that could inflict mass death throughout the region.

In 1990, after Iraq's invasion of Kuwait, the world imposed economic sanctions on Iraq. Those sanctions were maintained after the war to compel the regime's compliance with Security Council resolutions. In time, Iraq was allowed to use oil revenues to buy food. Saddam Hussein has subverted this program, working around the sanctions to buy missile technology and military materials. He blames the suffering of Iraq's people on the United Nations, even as he uses his oil wealth to build lavish palaces for himself, and arms his country. By refusing to comply with his own agreements, he bears full guilt for the hunger and misery of innocent Iraqi citizens.

In 1991, Iraq promised U.N. inspectors immediate and unrestricted access to verify Iraq's commitment to rid itself of weapons of mass destruction and long-range missiles. Iraq broke this promise, spending seven years deceiving, evading and harassing U.N. inspectors before ceasing cooperation entirely. Just months after the 1991 cease-fire, the Security Council twice renewed its demand that the Iraqi regime cooperate fully with inspectors, "condemning" Iraq's "serious violations" of its obligations. The Security Council again renewed that demand in 1994 and twice more in 1996, "deploring" Iraq's "clear violations" of its obligations. The Security Council renewed its demand three more times in 1997, citing "flagrant violations" and three more times in 1998, calling Iraq's behavior "totally unacceptable." And in 1999, the demand was renewed yet again.

As we meet today, it has been almost four years since the last U.N. inspectors set foot in Iraq—four years for the Iraqi regime to plan and build and test behind a cloak of secrecy. We know that Saddam Hussein pursued weapons of mass murder even when inspectors were in the country. Are we to assume that he stopped when they left? The history, the logic and the facts lead to one conclusion. Saddam Hussein's regime is a grave and gathering danger. To suggest otherwise is to hope against the evidence. To assume this regime's good faith is to bet the lives of millions and the peace of the world in a reckless gamble. And this is a risk we must not take.

Will the U.N. Stop Hussein or Be Irrelevant?

Delegates to the General Assembly: We have been more than patient. We have tried sanctions. We have tried the carrot of "oil for food" and the stick of coalition military strikes. But Saddam Hussein has defied all these efforts and continues to develop weapons of mass destruction. The first time we may be completely certain he has nuclear weapons is when, God forbid, he uses one. We owe it to all our citizens to do everything in our power to prevent that day from coming.

The conduct of the Iraqi regime is a threat to the authority of the United Nations, and a threat to peace. Iraq has answered a decade of U.N. demands with a decade of defiance. All the world now faces a test and the United Nations a difficult and defining moment. Are Security Council resolutions to be honored and enforced or cast aside without consequence? Will the United Nations serve the purpose of its founding or will it be irrelevant?

The United States helped found the United Nations. We want the U.N. to be effective and respected and successful. We want the resolutions of the world's most important multilateral body to be enforced. Right now these resolutions are being unilaterally subverted by the Iraqi regime. Our partnership of nations can meet the test before us, by making clear what we now expect of the Iraqi regime.

If the Iraqi regime wishes peace, it will immediately and

unconditionally forswear, disclose and remove or destroy all weapons of mass destruction, long-range missiles and all related material.

If the Iraqi regime wishes peace, it will immediately end all support for terrorism and act to suppress it, as all states are required to do by U.N. Security Council resolutions.

If the Iraqi regime wishes peace, it will cease persecution of its civilian population, including Shi'a, Sunnis, Kurds, Turkomans and others—again as required by Security Council resolutions.

If the Iraqi regime wishes peace, it will release or account for all Gulf War personnel whose fate is still unknown. It will return the remains of any who are deceased, return stolen property, accept liability for losses resulting from the invasion of Kuwait, and fully cooperate with international efforts to resolve these issues—as required by the Security Council resolutions.

If the Iraqi regime wishes peace, it will immediately end all illicit trade outside the oil-for-food program. It will accept U.N. administration of funds from that program, to ensure that the money is used fairly and promptly for the benefit of the Iraqi people.

If all these steps are taken, it will signal a new openness and accountability in Iraq. And it could open the prospect of the United Nations helping to build a government that represents all Iraqis—a government based on respect for human rights, economic liberty and internationally supervised elections.

The United States has no quarrel with the Iraqi people, who have suffered for too long in silent captivity. Liberty for the Iraqi people is a great moral cause and a great strategic goal. The people of Iraq deserve it and the security of all nations requires it. Free societies do not intimidate through cruelty and conquest and open societies do not threaten the world with mass murder. The United States supports political and economic liberty in a unified Iraq.

We can harbor no illusions. Saddam Hussein attacked Iran in 1980, and Kuwait in 1990. He has fired ballistic missiles at Iran, Saudi Arabia, Bahrain and Israel. His regime once ordered the killing of every person between the ages of 15 and 70 in certain Kurdish villages in Northern Iraq. He has gassed many Iranians and 40 Iraqi villages. My nation will work with the U.N. Security Council on a new resolution to meet our common challenge. If Iraq's regime defies us again, the world must move deliberately and decisively to hold Iraq to account. The purposes of the United States should not be doubted. The Security Council resolutions will be enforced—the just demands of peace and security will be met—or action will be unavoidable. And a regime that has lost its legitimacy will also lose its power. Events can turn in one of two ways.

If we fail to act in the face of danger, the people of Iraq will continue to live in brutal submission. The regime will have new power to bully, dominate and conquer its neighbors, condemning the Middle East to more years of bloodshed and fear. The region will remain unstable, with little hope of freedom and isolated from the progress of our times. With every step the Iraqi regime takes toward gaining and deploying the most terrible weapons, our own options to confront that regime will narrow. And if an emboldened regime were to supply these weapons to terrorist allies, then the attacks of September 11th would be a prelude to far greater horrors.

If we meet our responsibilities, if we overcome this danger, we can arrive at a very different future. The people of Iraq can shake off their captivity. They can one day join a democratic Afghanistan and a democratic Palestine, inspiring reforms throughout the Muslim world. These nations can show by their example that honest government, and respect for women, and the great Islamic tradition of learning can triumph in the Middle East and beyond. And we will show that the promise of the United Nations can be fulfilled in our time.

Neither of these outcomes is certain. Both have been set before us. We must choose between a world of fear and a world of progress. We cannot stand by and do nothing while dangers gather. We must stand up for our security, and for the permanent rights and hopes of mankind. By heritage and by choice, the United States of America will make that stand. Delegates to the United Nations, you have the power to make that stand as well.

American Aggression in Iraq Will Fail

Saddam Hussein

President Bush, in his January 29, 2002, "axis of evil"
speech, identified Iraq as a country that threatens the
peace of the world because of its support of terror and its
efforts to develop weapons of mass destruction. In his
September 12, 2002, speech to the United Nations (UN),
Bush made a strong case for UN intervention and renewal of weapons inspections in Iraq, leading to efforts
by UN Security Council members to develop a new resolution on weapons inspections and enforcement in the
event of Iraq's noncompliance.

Saddam Hussein immediately agreed to allow the return of inspectors under old UN rules, which limited inspectors and prevented inspections of presidential
palaces, but the United States pressed for stronger requirements. Initially, Hussein refrained from directly re-
sponding to the U.S. anti-Iraq rhetoric, but in a speech on
August 8, 2002, marking the fourteenth anniversary of
the Iran-Iraq War, Hussein warned that aggressors on
Iraqi soil would be "buried in their own coffin" of evil.

In October 2002, Hussein was reelected to seven
more years as president of Iraq; notably, however, Hussein's name was the only one on the ballot, and the election took place in a dictatorship where any display of disloyalty to Hussein can result in imprisonment or even
death. In the following speech, made by Hussein at his
swearing-in ceremony on October 21, 2002, Hussein
refers directly to America as a "Zionist tyrant" and

Saddam Hussein, speech before a Joint Session of Revolution Command Council
and the National Assembly in Iraq, October 21, 2002.

claims the United States is choosing the "road of blood and violence" after September 11, 2001, instead of reconsidering its Middle East policies.

"Nay, we hurl the truth against
Falsehood, and it knocks out its brain,
And behold, falsehood doth perish"
(Allah's is the word of truth)
Our great, loyal, and faithful People of Mujahideen,
Our valiant men and women,
Our heroes of the armed forces,
Our Arab Brethren,
Our friends,
Assalamu alaykum,

Seven years ago, on an occasion as this one, though under different circumstances, we met also here on the sacred, proud and generous land of Iraq, the land of God, our land which the Almighty has graced with His blessing, and has made its people proud and healthy when it so wants and maintains its true path of faith, in order to build this land, protect it, and defend its holy places.

The American Tyrant Misleads the People

We met on an occasion like this seven years ago, and we meet now to honor and celebrate a similar occasion seven years later. We met seven years ago to honor and celebrate the phenomenon and results of the Great March, and we meet today also to honor and celebrate this Great Pledge of Allegiance. So, here are the brothers and friends who have come to be present amongst us in Iraq and to see the festivities of the Iraqi people and the capacity of the Iraqi challenge in expressing itself and its position in a new field. This is the field in which many have been defeated, and many peoples have failed to express their true position and identity, having failed to find guidance to the right path at the right moment of time for the stand taken, especially when American tyranny, before it and its rear-lackeys were exposed, as they have been today, for what they really are, had projected themselves as if it were trying to help peoples to voice their positions in a democratic manner. Indeed, the American tyrant and its league of followers succeeded in misleading the peoples and the rulers whom they were able to deceive, so that they would neither find themselves, nor the right way in which to express their position in a proper and original manner. This happened when they were able to isolate the people from its leadership, or when the people's rulers failed to discharge their leadership effectively, honestly and responsibly. The tyrant then assumed full control over the people, and controlled their rulers or leaders, having first weakened, then isolated, them from their peoples.

As for the people of Iraq, they have demonstrated before you, in a candid and transparent manner, twice over the past seven years, a new level of awareness, and presented mankind with a visual and tangible picture of two Great Marches on the road of free expression. The people have also shown the level of closeness reached in the relationship between them and their leadership. The people's awareness, resolve and potential are such that, with reliance on Allah and self-confidence, strengthened by divine guidance for them and their leadership, they have come to take the right road and have reached their destination, enjoying the fruitful outcome of their efforts and sacrifices, and their self-control, resilience and patience.

But if anyone amongst you wishes to ask why the people of Iraq have achieved victory even in this field of the battle, which is a great victory over the enemies and an expression of both self and stance, then the answer will not only be found in the history of the Iraqi people and their relationship with their leadership since the July Revolution of 1968, but also in the bright and glorious history of the civilizations of Iraq and in seven thousand years of recorded history on this land since the first step in writing, in law, the arts, industry and agriculture, in the capacity to confront the enemies, and in the honor bestowed by Allah the Gracious upon this land by making it home for the inspiration and birth of the first prophesy which delivered the great meanings of guidance for the human race: "Never could we have found guidance, had it not been for the guidance of Allah."

America Should Reconsider Its Policies

Brothers and friends,

You too are facing, each in his or her field, the coercion and evil brought by the futile policies of the United States. I believe you wish to see the US officials reconsider their policies towards other nations and people, as we wished them to do so in open letters addressed to them after the bloody events of the eleventh September, 2001. These were probably the wishes of other rulers and leaders as well as of other nations and peoples through their scholars and analysts who seek to identify the causes and find successful solutions. But, as the Almighty says: "Thou canst not make the dead listen, nor canst thou cause the deaf to hear the call."

And as the Arab poet said:

"The living would have heard your call,
But those you call on are lifeless."

America Has Chosen the Road of Blood and Violence

The Americans did not hear the call. They found it easier to take the road of blood and violence. Their means of destruction gave them arrogance. So they decided to pursue this road rather than search for the causes in order to know the connection between the phenomena and their outcome, and determine what remedy to prescribe, in order that security and peace may prevail, and justice and fairness be achieved.

The road of blood can only lead to more blood. We have learnt this fact from our elders in the countryside. We used to hear them say it many years ago, despite their simple life of limited education, which means that this is a law of life, a law of human relationship not only in Iraq. The road of blood takes you to more blood; and he who tries to shed the blood of others must expect his blood to be spilled.

The American administrations have for long been the product of the games of the Zionist lobby in the United

States. They cannot see the facts as they are; and even if they did see the facts as they were, they would not be able to act according to their own interpretation, but only according to the interests of the Zionist lobby and the Zionist entity which occupies Palestine. Therefore, save the world from the evils of the American administration whose aggressions is fueled by the Zionist alliance with big business and special influential interests, will spare the peoples of the United States the animosities, tragedies and sacrifices created by their administrations, especially the current administration, thus affecting them and the world at large, including the region in which we live, the Middle East, and the Nation of which we are part, our glorious Arab Nation. This can only be averted when the American people takes up its role in accordance with a humane outlook based on a desire for peace, stability, cooperation and fairness, with the support of the European nations, each according to its own experience, presenting advice by tangible examples derived from their relations with other peoples of the world, including the peoples of the Middle East, in the forefront of which comes our glorious Arab Nation. In addition to this, there is the resilience of those aggressed against by the alliance between Zionism and those administrations. This resilience is supported by freedom lovers all over the world, representing its effective human depth, and causing the arrows of aggression to go astray, thus helping to achieve security and stability, peace, fairness and cooperation.

To the brothers and friends who have come to Iraq I say:

I salute you and appreciate, in the name of the people of Iraq, the journey you have endured to come here and be with us on this occasion. I thank you for your appreciation of our people, your solidarity with it in defending its heritage, faith, existence, honor and sanctities in the face of those who hate humanity, and are therefore hated, isolated by humanity.

Appendix of Biographies

Yasser Arafat

Yasser Arafat was born in Cairo, Egypt, on August 24, 1929, as Mohammed Rahman Abdel-Raouf Arafat al Qudwa al-Hussein. His parents were Palestinian; his father was a textile merchant. Arafat's mother died when he was five years old, and he apparently was not close to his father, who died in 1952. He appears to have been raised by his uncle and later by his older sister. He attended the University of Faud I (later Cairo University), majored in engineering, and acquired his degree in 1956. After college, Arafat worked in Egypt, then in Kuwait, where he was employed in the department of public works, and later founded his own contracting firm. Arafat's personal life is kept fairly secret, but he is married to Suha Tawil and has a daughter, Zahwa.

While he was still a teenager, Arafat became involved with the Palestinian struggle against the British and the Jews in Palestine. At the University of Faud, he was leader of the Palestinian students, and after graduation, he spent all his spare time on political matters. In 1958 Arafat founded Al-Fatah, a group dedicated to armed struggle against Israel. At the end of 1964, Arafat left Kuwait, moved to Jordan, and began working full time with Al-Fatah.

The Palestine Liberation Organization (PLO) was created by the Arab League to bring together groups working for Palestinian independence, including Al-Fatah, although the PLO's policy was more moderate than Al-Fatah's. In 1969, following Israel's victory in the 1967 Six-Day War, Arafat became the chairman of the PLO executive committee. At this point, the PLO changed from an organization controlled by the Arab states to an independent Palestinian organization based in Jordan. Under Arafat's direction, the PLO in Jordan developed its own military forces and launched guerrilla attacks on Israel. When Jordan expelled the PLO for its violent activities, Arafat relocated the PLO first to Lebanon, and then to Tunis, where he continued the PLO terrorist strikes on Israel. In 1974 Arafat was invited to address the United Nations; he called on the world community to view the PLO not as terrorists but as freedom fighters resisting Israeli occupation and oppression.

In 1988 Arafat signaled a PLO policy shift from terrorism to diplomacy, renouncing terrorism and recognizing for the first time Israel's right to exist. Thereafter, Arafat pursued peace negotiations, signing a peace agreement with Israel in 1993 called the Oslo Accords, a feat that brought Arafat, Israeli prime minister Yitzhak Rabin, and Israeli foreign minister Shimon Peres the Nobel Peace Prize. This agreement provided for Palestinian self-rule, and Arafat thereafter was elected president of the newly created Palestine Authority.

Since 1996, however, Israel's right-wing leadership, under Benjamin Netanyahu and later Ariel Sharon, together with increased Palestinian terrorist strikes, have slowed the peace process. Also, in 1999, to the disappointment of Israel and many observers, Arafat rejected a peace proposal from Israel that offered the Palestinians a sovereign state with control over much of the territory in the West Bank, excluding Jerusalem. Since then, more radical Palestinian resistance groups (such as Hamas, Palestinian Islamic Jihad, and Hezbollah) have increased suicide terrorist attacks on Israel, threatening Arafat's vision of a secular Palestinian state living side by side with Israel. In 2002 Israel, under the leadership of Sharon, placed Arafat under house arrest for failing to stop continuing Palestinian terrorist strikes against Israeli civilians. Israel's targeting of Arafat, however, has had the effect of increasing his status among Arabs. Indeed, Arafat is known for his ability to survive both political and life-threatening events, including an airplane crash, assassination attempts by Israel, and a serious stroke.

Menachem Begin

Menachem Begin was born in Brisk (now Brest-Litovsk), Poland, then part of the Russian Empire, on August 16, 1913. He was the youngest of three children born to Zev Dov and Hassia Begin. The family was forced to leave Poland to escape the fighting between the German and Russian armies during World War I. After the war, Begin returned to Poland with his family. There, he completed high school, enrolled in Warsaw University in 1931, and earned a law degree in 1935. Begin later married and had a son and two daughters.

After graduation, Begin worked with the Betar Zionist, the nationalist youth movement associated with the Zionist Revisionist Movement, and in 1939 became head of the Polish Betar organization, fighting against British policy in Palestine. At the beginning of World War II, Begin was arrested by the Russian authorities and was imprisoned in concentration camps in Siberia and elsewhere, until he was released in 1941. Begin then joined the Polish army and was assigned to the Middle East. His parents and older brother remained in Poland and died during the Holocaust.

Shortly after his move to Israel in 1942, Begin agreed to assume command of the Irgun Zvati Leumi (National Military Organization), a terrorist organization advocating armed struggle against British rule in Israel. By the end of 1943, the extent of the Holocaust and its effect on European Jews were beginning to be understood, but the British government refused to permit further Jewish immigration to Israel, adhering to the policy of the White Paper (the British official policy paper adopted in 1939 that restricted Jewish immigration to Israel to ensure that Jews would not constitute more than one-third of the population of Palestine). As a result, Begin concluded that there was no alternative to a war against the British rule in Israel, and on February 1, 1944, the Irgun distributed flyers entitled "Proclamation of the Revolt," announcing the beginning of its terror campaign.

Thereafter, the Irgun staged numerous attacks on British government facilities, each more daring than the last. One of the most famous attacks was in July 1946 at the King David Hotel, the headquarters of British military and civilian administration in Palestine; the bomb killed ninety-one people and injured forty-five, including both Arab and Jewish civilians. Ultimately, the organization's terror campaign was successful in driving the British out of Israel, and the United Nations voted to separate Palestine into separate Jewish and Palestinian areas, creating the state of Israel in 1948. Begin spoke in defense of his group's armed struggle against the British at that time, and he later wrote a book about his Irgun activities called *The Revolt*.

Thereafter, Begin founded the Herut Party, which later became the Likud Party. On June 20, 1977, Begin won the Knesset elections and became prime minister of Israel. As prime minister, Begin initiated peace talks with Arab countries and signed the Camp David Accords in 1978, which set the stage for a 1979 Egypt–Israel peace treaty. In December 1978 Prime Minister Begin and Egyptian president Anwar Sadat were jointly awarded the Nobel Peace Prize. On June 30, 1981, Begin was reelected prime minister. Following the death of his wife in 1982, Begin resigned from government and spent the rest of his life in seclusion. He died in 1992.

Osama bin Laden

Osama bin Laden, the leader of the terrorist group al-Qaeda and now the leading suspect in the September 11, 2001, attacks on America, was born in Saudi Arabia in 1957 to a wealthy family. His father, Mohammed bin Laden, founded a construction company that, due to its royal connections, acquired numerous important projects, earning billions. Mohammed bin Laden took numerous wives and fathered about fifty children; Osama was the seventeenth son, born to a wife of Syrian background. Bin Laden studied management and economics at King Abdul Aziz University in Jedda, Saudi Arabia. As a result of his later terrorist activities, bin Laden has been disowned by most of his family.

In 1979 the Soviets invaded Afghanistan, and bin Laden moved to Afghanistan and supported the Afghan resistance, or mujahideen. In this effort, bin Laden was aligned with the United States, which also opposed the Soviet Union and funded the Islamic mujahideen. During this period, bin Laden recruited Islamic soldiers from around the globe. After the Soviet army withdrew in 1989, the fundamentalist Taliban government was formed to quell factional fighting, and bin Laden returned to Saudi Arabia.

Soon, however, bin Laden became angry that the Saudi government allowed the United States to station troops in Saudi Arabia in 1990 as part of Operation Desert Storm, the U.S. military response to Iraq's invasion of Kuwait. He accused the Saudi government of straying from Islam, and in 1991 bin Laden was expelled from Saudi Arabia and his Saudi citizenship was revoked. He next moved to Sudan, where he worked with Egyptian radical groups. As a result of U.S. and Saudi Arabia pressure, however, Sudan expelled bin Laden, and in 1996 he returned to Afghanistan, where the Taliban provided sanctuary.

During this period of the 1980s and 1990s, bin Laden developed thousands of followers, founded his terrorist organization (al-Qaeda, or "the Base"), and used his estimated $250-million fortune to fund large-scale terrorist actions. Bin Laden and al-Qaeda have been implicated in a number of such terrorist attacks on the United States, including the 1993 World Trade Center bombing, the 1998 bombings at the U.S. embassies in Kenya and Tanzania, and the 2000 bombing of the USS *Cole* in Yemen. Bin Laden also has claimed responsibility for a 1993 incident in Somalia that killed eighteen U.S. soldiers and a 1996 bombing of the Khobar military complex in Saudi Arabia that killed nineteen U.S. personnel. In 1998 bin Laden called publicly for all Americans and Jews to be killed. He is believed to be seeking nuclear or chemical weapons. Ironically, bin Laden is regarded by many in the Arab world as a hero for his support of radical Islam and the Palestinian cause and for his attacks on the United States and Israel.

After the September 11, 2001, attack on the United States, and the Taliban's refusal to turn over bin Laden and his fellow terrorists, the United States and Britain launched a military strike on Afghanistan in October 2002 that quickly toppled the Taliban regime. Bin Laden, however, has never been caught, and it is unclear whether he is dead or alive. He has appeared in several video-tapes broadcast on Qatar's Al-Jazeera television network, the first of which praised the September 11 terrorist action. In later tapes, in November and December 2001, bin Laden appears to claim responsibility for the attacks and threatens future actions.

Tony Blair

Tony Blair was born in Scotland in May 1953, and went to school at Durham and Edinburgh. He studied law at Oxford University and qualified as a barrister in London in 1976. While at Oxford, he also was an actor, an athlete, and the lead singer of the rock band Ugly Rumours. Later, in his law career, he specialized in employment law. In 1980 he married Cherie Booth, a lawyer; they have four children.

In 1983 Tony Blair was elected to Parliament, where he held several posts, including opposition spokesman on treasury and economic affairs (1984–1987), opposition spokesman on trade and industry (1987–1988), shadow secretary of state for energy (1988–1989), shadow secretary of state for employment (1989–1992), and opposition spokesman on home affairs. In 1994 he became leader of the Labour Party, with the goal of turning the minority party into a more centrist entity that would be able to win general elections.

In 1997 Blair succeeded in his goal and was elected Britain's prime minister in a landslide, at the young age of forty-four. His political platform supported a tough but liberal crime policy, a free-market economy with an emphasis on anti-inflationary tactics, and Britain's participation in the European Community. He abandoned more traditional Labour Party issues, such as support for unions, welfare, and nuclear disarmament.

George W. Bush

George Walker Bush was born July 6, 1946, in New Haven, Connecticut, the eldest son of George and Barbara Bush. He came from a prominent political family—his grandfather Prescott Bush had been a senator from Connecticut. In 1948 the family moved to Texas, where the senior George Bush worked in the oil business and made his fortune. Bush grew up in Texas in the shadow of his famous father, who was active in politics and became a U.S. congressman, political appointee, and eventually president of the United States.

The younger Bush graduated from Yale with a history degree in 1968, and thereafter joined the Texas Air National Guard as a pilot, which allowed him to avoid military service in Vietnam. In 1973 Bush entered Harvard Business School, graduating with an MBA in 1975. He then returned to Texas, where he established his own oil and gas business during the late 1970s. In 1977 he met and married Laura Welch, a librarian. The couple has twin daughters, Jenna and Barbara, born in 1981.

Due to his family's political background, Bush was immersed in politics from an early age. In 1977 Bush decided to run for the U.S. Congress; he won the Republican primary, but he lost the general election. He then returned to the oil business but failed to achieve in this field as his father had. When his company, Spectrum 7, was about to collapse in 1985, it was acquired by a Dallas firm and Bush fortuitously wound up with a seat on the board and $300,000 in company stock.

In 1986 Bush, who had a history of drinking too much, gave up alcohol and renewed his Christian faith. Later, he became a paid adviser to his father's successful 1988 presidential campaign. Next, Bush assembled a group of investors to purchase the Texas Rangers baseball franchise in 1989; although Bush invested only $606,302, he was named managing partner, a position that helped him to build a reputation with the public as a businessman. The team was sold in 1998 for $250 million, earning Bush $14.9 million on his $606,302 investment.

Finally, in 1993, after his father's unsuccessful bid for reelection, Bush ran for and won the Texas governorship, beating popular incumbent Ann Richards. He was reelected in 1998. Bush then announced his candidacy for the 2000 presidential election, characterizing himself as a "compassionate conservative," but otherwise following the traditional conservative line of small government, tax cuts, a strong military, and opposition to gun control and abortion.

Bush's presidency to date, however, has been defined largely by the events of the terrorist attack on September 11, 2001. Since then, his administration has focused on the war in Afghanistan and the search for Osama bin Laden and al-Qaeda terrorists. Most recently, Bush has threatened to attack Iraq to destroy the regime of Saddam Hussein in order to prevent him from acquiring weapons of mass destruction. Bush's zeal for attacking Iraq, however, and his policy change from a defensive international posture to one of preemptive, unilateral military attacks on terrorist threats, has engendered much opposition, both domestically and around the world. Apparently in response to this criticism, Bush has sought United Nations (UN) authorization for military action against Iraq in the event of Iraq's noncooperation with renewed weapons inspections.

Bill Clinton

Bill Clinton was born on August 19, 1946, in Hope, Arkansas, as William Jefferson Blythe IV. His father died in a car accident three months before he was born, and when he was two years old, his mother left him with his grandparents while she pursued nursing studies. His mother married Roger Clinton and reunited the family when Bill was four years old, and he took the name Clinton when he was in high school. Although he played the saxophone and once considered becoming a professional musician, Clinton excelled in school, and at age sixteen he was inspired by a meeting with President John F. Kennedy to enter politics. Clinton met President Kennedy as a delegate to the American Legion Boy's Nation program in Washington, D.C. Thereafter, Clinton graduated from Georgetown University, in 1968 won a Rhodes scholarship to Oxford University, and received a law degree from Yale University in 1973. While in law school, Clinton met Hillary Rodham, his future wife.

After law school, Clinton moved back to Arkansas with Hillary and entered politics. He ran for but was defeated in his Democratic campaign for Congress in Arkansas's Third District in 1974. The following year he married Hillary, and the couple had a child, Chelsea, in 1980. In 1976 Clinton won his first state election when he was elected Arkansas's attorney general. Two years later, in 1978, Clinton was elected governor of Arkansas and became the nation's youngest governor. Clinton and his staff of young liberal activists, however, alienated both conservative Arkansas voters and several powerful special interests, leading to his defeat in the 1980 gubernatorial election. This defeat motivated Clinton to become more moderate and pragmatic, and he regained the governorship in 1982 and retained it for five consecutive terms.

In 1990 Clinton became chairman of the Democratic Leadership Council, which rated him as the most effective governor in the country. In 1992 Clinton ran for president and defeated Republican incumbent George Bush and third-party candidate Ross Perot, largely by emphasizing economic issues. Clinton's presidency marked the arrival of a new baby-boom generation in Washington and the first time in twelve years that the same party controlled both the executive and legislative branches of government. Although Clinton presided over a period of unprecedented peace and prosperity in the United States, including the creation of a federal budget surplus, he was unable to achieve his goal of a national health care policy.

In 1994 the Democrats lost control of both houses of Congress, leading to a stalemate between conservative Republican legislators and the White House and to a number of congressional investigations into Clinton's business and personal dealings. For example, Congress investigated but never proved alleged improprieties by the president during a 1980s Arkansas land deal called Whitewater. Also, in 1998, as a result of sexual indiscretions with a White House intern, Clinton became the second U.S. president to be impeached by the House of Representatives. He was tried in the Senate but found not guilty of the charges brought against him. Despite these events, however, Clinton enjoyed unprecedented popular-approval ratings as president. Clinton was president in 1995 when a right-wing domestic terrorist, Timothy McVeigh, bombed a government building in Oklahoma City, killing 168 persons; in response, Clinton proposed counter terrorism legislation to provide federal law enforcement officials with better tools to combat terrirosm. In 1996 he was reelected by a comfortable margin over Republican nominee Robert Dole, and his vice president, Al Gore, became the Democratic nominee during the 2000 election against George W. Bush.

Michael Collins

Michael Collins was born on October 16, 1890, in West Cork, Ireland, to a farming family. As a young man, he developed an early pride about his Irish ancestry from teachers and others, and when he was a teenager he became a member of the Irish Republican Brotherhood (IRB), a revolutionary group working for Irish independence from British rule. He spent his early youth working in London, but he returned to Ireland in 1916 to take part in the Irish fight for freedom as a captain in the Irish Volunteers, a group planning an insurrection against the British. He was imprisoned briefly, and when he was released, he quickly became immersed in the work of liberating Ireland.

The IRB and the Volunteers ultimately became part of a rebel group called Sinn Fein, and Collins became the commander of its military, the Irish Republican Army (IRA). Between 1916 and 1922, he developed an intelligence network, smuggled arms, coordinated an assassination squad, and orchestrated a terror campaign against the British military in Ireland. One of the most famous incidents, called Bloody Sunday, occurred on November 21, 1920, when British troops fired on a crowd watching a football match, killing twelve, in retaliation for Collins's assassination of British intelligence officers.

By 1921 the violence had demoralized the British, a truce was declared, and treaty talks began between the two sides. Collins was appointed one of the IRA's chief negotiators, but the talks resulted in a treaty that provided less than full and complete Irish independence. The treaty plunged Ireland into a bloody civil war between those who followed Collins and the anti-treaty forces, known as the Irregulars. On August 22, 1922, shortly after the signing of the treaty and after the civil war had begun, Michael Collins was ambushed by an unknown assassin while in his home county visiting troops; he died at the age of thirty-two. Collins is remembered as a beloved Irish patriot who laid the groundwork for Ireland to eventually win its independence from British rule.

Charles de Gaulle

Charles de Gaulle was born on November 22, 1890, the second son of an upper-middle-class French Roman Catholic family. His father taught philosophy and literature. De Gaulle showed an early interest in military matters, and he attended the Military Academy of Saint-Cyr.

In 1913 de Gaulle became a second lieutenant in an infantry regiment. He fought, was wounded three times, and spent almost three years as a prisoner during World War I. In 1925 he was promoted to the staff of the French Conseil Supérieur de la Guerre (Supreme War Council). Later, he served as a major in the army occupying the Rhineland against German aggression. He also spent two years in the Middle East and then, having been promoted to lieutenant colonel, spent four years as a member of the secretariat of the Conseil Supérieur de la Défense Nationale (National Defense Council). During World War II, de Gaulle commanded a tank brigade attached to the French Fifth Army, and in 1940 he was made a temporary brigadier general in the Fourth Armoured Division, a post that allowed him to develop theories of modern armored warfare.

On June 6, 1940, de Gaulle became undersecretary of state for defense and war under the government of Paul Reynaud, which refused to surrender to German invasion forces. When the government was replaced with one that agreed to an armistice with the Germans, de Gaulle left for England and appealed to the French to continue their fight against Germany. On August 2, 1940, a French military court tried him and sentenced him to death in absentia. De Gaulle, however, became the leader of the "Free French," recognized by Britain as the last legitimate French government, and the British assisted his plan for resistance to the pro-German Vichy government in France. Thereafter, de Gaulle's forces played an important role in the liberation of France and the defeat of Nazi Germany, and de Gaulle was viewed by the French as a hero.

After the war, an insurrection by native Muslims in the French colony of Algiers threatened to bring civil war to France. In 1955, a resistance group called Front de Liberation Nationale (FLN) began a campaign of terror aimed at winning independence from French rule. French settlers in the area, known as colons, fought the FLN and called for the return of de Gaulle to power, believing he would effectively stem the rebellion. In May 1958 de Gaulle returned as prime minister of France, and in December of that year he was elected president and given new powers for ruling in a state of emergency. De Gaulle, however, recognized that France's colonial rule in Algiers had to end. In a 1959 speech, he declared that Algerians had the right to self-determination, leading to a peace agreement in 1962 that resulted in independence for Algeria and ended the seven-year Algerian war.

De Gaulle was reelected to a second presidential term in 1965, but in the following years he lost the support of the French voters when he withdrew from the North Atlantic Treaty Organization (NATO) and followed what were viewed as anti-American policies. In 1969, following his defeat in a presidential referendum, de Gaulle resigned and retired to writing. He died of a heart attack in 1970.

Emma Goldman

Emma Goldman was born to a Jewish family in Russia in 1869; she would grow up to become one of the most well-known advocates of anarchism, free speech, women's rights, and birth control. She emigrated to the United States when she was sixteen, where she found work in a Rochester, New York, garment factory. In 1889 she moved to New York City, became active in the anarchist movement, and met fellow-Russian anarchist and lifelong companion Alexander Berkman. The anarchists fought against repressive government and believed in the "propaganda of the deed," that is, in the use of terrorist tactics to bring attention to their cause. In the United States, anarchists became involved in the early labor movement.

In her younger years, Goldman advocated violence. She was influenced by a labor incident in May 1886 in Haymarket Square in Chicago; during a workers' protest of police violence, a bomb was thrown, killing seven police officers, and prominent anarchists and organizers of the protest were found responsible and executed. In 1892, in retaliation for the Carnegie Steel Company's shooting of nine striking steelworkers, she helped Berkman plot to assassinate industrialist Henry Clay Frick. Berkman failed in the assassination attempt, and he was caught and sent to prison; Goldman was never charged.

Later, Goldman rejected terrorism and instead dedicated herself to political organizing and advocating her version of the anarchist cause. Goldman became involved in various free speech and civil liberties issues and was known as a great advocate of women's rights and birth control. She was a skilled speaker and writer, and her books included *Anarchism and Other Essays, The Social Significance of the Modern Drama, My Disillusionment in Russia,* and *Living My Life.*

The U.S. government, however, pursued her for her radical activities and nicknamed her "Red Emma." She was jailed on several occasions, and in 1908 she was deprived of her U.S. citizenship. In 1917 Goldman and Berkman were tried and later imprisoned for protesting military conscription for World War I. In a July 9, 1917, speech to the jury during the trial, Goldman defended herself against conspiracy charges and claims that she supported political violence.

Ultimately, at the height of the post–World War I anti-Communist fervor in the United States in 1919, the government deported both Goldman and Berkman to Russia. They left the Soviet Union after a short time, however, profoundly disillusioned with the new Bolshevik authoritarian state. Goldman spent the last part of her life traveling and lecturing in France, England, and Canada; she died in 1940 of a stroke.

Thomas Graham Jr.

Thomas Graham Jr. was born in Louisville, Kentucky, and attended public high school there, graduating in 1951. He acquired his undergraduate degree in 1955 from Princeton University, where he studied international relations; he graduated from Harvard Law School with a bachelor of laws degree in 1961. Graham is married to Christine Coffey Ryan and has three children and two stepchildren.

Graham served as general counsel, acting director, and acting deputy director of the U.S. Arms Control and Disarmament Agency (ACDA) from 1977 to 1981 and from 1983 to 1994. His assignments included serving as the legal adviser to the U.S. SALT II delegation (1974–1979), the senior arms control agency representative to the U.S. Intermediate-Range Nuclear Forces delegation (1981–1982), the legal adviser to the U.S. Nuclear and Space Arms delegation (1985–1988), the senior arms control agency representative and legal adviser to the U.S. delegation to the Conventional Armed Forces in Europe Negotiation (1989–1990). He also served as the legal adviser to the U.S. delegation to the Non-Proliferation

Treaty Review Conference in 1980, the legal adviser to the U.S. delegation to the 1988 ABM Treaty Review Conference, the legal adviser to the U.S. START I delegation in 1991, and the legal adviser to the U.S. START II delegation in 1992–1993.

From 1994 to 1997, Graham served as the special representative of the president for arms control, nonproliferation, and disarmament. In this position, he led U.S. government efforts to achieve a permanent Nuclear Non-Proliferation Treaty (NPT) leading up to and during the 1995 Review and Extension Conference of the NPT. Graham headed the U.S. delegation to the 1996 Review Conference of the Conventional Armed Forces in Europe (CFE) Treaty, and the U.S. delegation to the 1993 ABM Treaty Review Conference. In addition, he led a number of delegations to foreign capitals between 1994 and 1996, first to persuade countries to support indefinite extension of the NPT and in 1996 to urge conclusion of the Comprehensive Test Ban Treaty (CTBT) negotiations in Geneva, Switzerland (the CTBT was signed in September 1996). In November 1995 and June 1996, Graham led a U.S. delegation to Indonesia to discuss with member states of the Association of Southeast Asian Nations (ASEAN) the emerging Southeast Asia Nuclear Free Zone Treaty.

Graham also worked on the negotiation of the Biological Weapons Convention and the Chemical Weapons Convention, and he managed the ratification of the Geneva Protocol banning the use in war of chemical and biological weapons and the Biological Weapons Convention. Graham drafted the implementing legislation of the Biological Weapons Convention (the law utilized by the Department of Justice to prevent biological weapons terrorism in the United States). On numerous occasions Ambassador Graham has testified before congressional committees on arms control and related issues. He has taught courses at the University of Virginia School of Law, the Georgetown School of Foreign Service, and the Georgetown University Law Center; has spoken widely on arms control issues around the country and abroad; and has chaired the American Bar Association Committee on Arms Control and Disarmament.

Graham next became the president of the Lawyers Alliance for World Security (LAWS), a nonpartisan, nongovernmental organization concerned with the proliferation of nuclear weapons and other weapons of mass destruction and committed to the pursuit of prudent arms control, nonproliferation, and disarmament efforts worldwide.

Saddam Hussein

Saddam Hussein was born on April 28, 1939, in Tikrit, Iraq, as a member of the Sunni Arab sect. His family was poor, and he was sent to live with his maternal uncle soon after he was born. In 1955 Hussein moved to Baghdad, and in 1956 he joined the Baath Party, a socialist Sunni Arab party with close Tikrit family and tribal ties, which was opposed to the colonial British monarchy that ruled Iraq at that time. The monarchy was overthrown in 1958 during a coup led by a military officer called Karim Qasim. In 1959 Hussein attempted, but failed, to assassinate Qasim, and thereafter Hussein fled to exile in Egypt and Syria.

In 1963 the Baath Party came to power briefly in Iraq, and Hussein returned to his homeland. The Baathists were quickly overthrown, however, and Hussein was imprisoned for a time until he escaped in 1967. In 1968 Hussein helped the Baath Party to again seize power during a coup led by his cousin Ahmed Hassan Bakr. For the next nine years, Hussein worked behind the scenes to become a key leader in the Baath Party. Among his duties was the development of a network of secret security police. In 1979 Hussein ousted Bakr to become president of Iraq. He quickly instituted a terror purge to rid the party of anyone who opposed him, consolidating his complete control over Iraq.

In 1979 the shah of Iran was overthrown by the Islamic Revolution, led by the Ayatollah Khomeini, and Hussein feared that the Islamic revolutionaries in Iran would trigger dissatisfied and disaffected Iraqi Shia Muslims to challenge the Baath Party's rule in Iraq. In 1980 Hussein attacked Iran, starting the prolonged Iran-Iraq War that lasted most of the decade. By the end of the war, Iraq possessed a strong military due to large amounts of aid from the West, including the United States.

After the war with Iraq, Hussein sought to rebuild Iraq economically. In 1990 Hussein accused Kuwait of driving down the price of oil by cheating on Organization of Petroleum Exporting Countries (OPEC) quotas and flooding the market. When Kuwait failed to agree to Hussein's demands for money and land, Iraq invaded Kuwait on August 2, 1990. Hussein refused to respond to United Nations (UN) resolutions calling for his withdrawal, and this resulted in a military strike on Iraq by the United States and its allies, UN weapons inspections, and more than a decade of UN economic sanctions that have crippled the Iraqi economy.

UN weapons inspections in Iraq ended in 1998, and since then, it is believed that Hussein has made every attempt to rebuild his weapons arsenal, including weapons of mass destruction—chemical, biological, and nuclear weapons. After the September 11, 2001, terrorist attack on the United States, U.S. president George W. Bush targeted Hussein's regime in Iraq as part of an "axis of evil," referring to states that sponsor terror and seek weapons of mass destruction. In 2002 Bush called on the United Nations to resume immediate and unconditional weapons inspections in Iraq and sought UN authorization for military action against Iraq if Hussein failed to fully cooperate with inspections and meet UN disarmament requirements. In August 2002 Hussein was reelected to another seven-year term as Iraq's president; his reelection was not given much credence in the West, however, because Hussein's name was the only name on the ballot and the state is known to crack down on anyone expressing disloyalty to Hussein in any form. Whether Hussein or his regime will survive the U.S. pressure remains to be seen.

Robert H. Jackson

Robert H. Jackson was born in 1892 in Spring Creek, Pennsylvania. He attended Albany law school briefly, and although he never acquired a law degree, he was admitted to the bar in 1913. In 1934 he became general counsel of the Bureau of Internal Revenue. From 1936 to 1938 he served as assistant attorney general in charge of the antitrust division.

In 1938 Jackson was appointed U.S. solicitor general by President Franklin D. Roosevelt. In 1940 he became the U.S. attorney general. Finally, in 1941, President Roosevelt appointed Jackson to the U.S. Supreme Court, where he served as associate justice from 1941 until 1954. Jackson's best-known decision was *West Virginia State Board of Education v. Barnette*, decided in 1943, which struck down laws that made saluting the flag mandatory for schoolchildren based on First Amendment, free speech grounds. Jackson was known for his eloquent literary style and his concern with freedom of religion.

In 1945, following World War II, President Roosevelt asked Jackson to take a leave from the Supreme Court bench to become the U.S. chief counsel at the Nuremberg war crimes trials. Jackson served in this capacity until 1946, after which he returned to the Supreme Court.

Jackson authored a number of books, including *The Struggle for Judicial Supremacy* (1940), *The Case Against the Nazi War Criminals* (1945), and *The Supreme Court in the American System of Government* (1955). He died in 1954.

Nikita Khrushchev

Nikita Khrushchev was born in 1894 in Kalinovka, Ukraine, the son of a peasant. He never finished elementary school, and he did not begin serious reading until he entered an adult training class at the age of twenty-seven. Throughout his life, Khrushchev would not be considered an intellectual but rather a man who loved contact with the common people. After Vladimir Lenin's Bolsheviks took control of the Russian government in 1917, Khrushchev joined the Bolshevik Party in 1918. Thereafter, he fought in the Russian civil war and rose rapidly in the party organization. In 1939 he was made a full member of the Politburo and of the Presidium of the Supreme Soviet.

In 1953, six months after the death of Joseph Stalin, Khrushchev became first secretary of the Communist Party of the Soviet Union. He built a base of support within the party, and three years later, at the Twentieth Party Congress, Khrushchev denounced Stalinism and the "personality cult" that Khrushchev claimed led to Stalin's brutal repression and terrorism of the Russian people. His denunciation of Stalin resulted in rebellion in Hungary; in 1956 Khrushchev brutally repressed the Hungarian uprising. Khrushchev also is famous for beating the United States in a race to send a rocket into space, when Russia successfully launched the *Sputnik* missiles in 1957. In 1962 Khrushchev brought the world to the brink of nuclear war when he attempted to install missiles in Cuba, leading to the infamous standoff with U.S. president John F. Kennedy during the Cuban Missile Crisis. In 1964 Khrushchev was ousted by Leonid Brezhnev and Aleksey Kosygin, and he went into retirement. He died in 1971.

Juan Miguel Linan Macias

Juan Miguel Linan Macias was born in Spain, in the province of Cordoba, in 1960. He entered the Higher Military Academy General Academy in 1979. From 1984 to 1989 he was assigned, as an officer, to Special Operations Units, and since 1989 he has served in Spain's Ministry of Defense as a Security and Counter-terrorism adviser and counselor. In addition to these duties, he currently takes part in several national and European bodies involved in the prevention of threats from international terrorism.

Sayyed Hasan Nassrallah

Sayyed Hasan Nassrallah is the secretary general of Hezbollah (meaning "Party of God"), an organization based in Lebanon viewed by the U.S. government as a terrorist group. Hezbollah began in 1982 with the assistance of revolutionary Iran to fight against the Israeli invasion of Lebanon. Since then, the group has established a cultural and political presence in Lebanon, operating schools and hospitals, and winning elections to become part of the Lebanese government. Hezbollah also is dedicated to the removal of Israel from Palestine and has conducted terrorist strikes against Israel. Nassrallah has been leading the party since 1991.

Benjamin Netanyahu

Benjamin Netanyahu was born on October 21, 1949, in Tel Aviv, Israel, and he grew up in Jerusalem. He lived in the United States during his high school years, where his father, Benzion Netanyahu, taught history. After high school, in 1967, Netanyahu joined Israel's defense forces and became an officer in an elite antiterror commando unit. He served in this position until 1972, during which he participated in a number of missions, including a rescue of hijacked hostages at Ben Gurion Airport, where he was wounded.

Thereafter, Netanyahu returned to the United States, where he studied at MIT and received degrees in architecture and management studies. He also studied political science at MIT and Harvard University. After college, he worked for the Boston Consulting Group, an international business consulting firm, and later he worked as a senior manager of Rim Industries in Jerusalem. Netanyahu married his wife, Sara, and is the father of Noa, Yair, and Avner.

In 1979 Netanyahu worked with a private foundation, the Jonathan Institute (named after his deceased brother, Jonathan), to organize an international conference against terrorism. Several world leaders took part in the conference and a later one in 1984, including former U.S. president George Bush and former secretary of state George Shultz.

In 1982 Netanyahu became deputy chief of mission in the Israeli Embassy in Washington, where he was a member of a delegation to talks on strategic cooperation between Israel and the United States. Two years later, in 1984, he was appointed Israel's ambassador to the United Nations. In 1988 Netanyahu returned to Israel and was elected to the Knesset (Israel's legislative body) as a right-wing Likud Party member and appointed deputy foreign minister.

In 1993 Netanyahu was elected Likud Party chairman and the party's candidate for prime minister. In 1996 Netanyahu was narrowly elected as prime minister, following the assassination of Prime Minister Yitshak Rabin, who had signed a peace agreement in 1993 (the Oslo Peace Accords) with the Palestinian terrorist group the Palestine Liberation Organization (PLO). During his time as prime minister, Israel's peace negotiations with the PLO slowed considerably. In 1998, however, Netanyahu met with PLO leader Yasser Arafat and agreed on a number of issues called for by the 1993 Oslo Peace Accords, including an agreement from the Palestinians to remove language from their founding charter that called for destroying Israel and a promise by Israel to withdraw from additional areas of the West Bank.

Following this meeting, Netanyahu was attacked by the right wing for giving up Israeli territory, and he later reneged on the promise to the PLO for Israeli withdrawals from the West Bank. In 1999 Labor Party leader Ehud Barak succeeded Netanyahu as prime minister, promising voters to revive the peace process with the PLO.

Netanyahu remains active in Israeli and international politics, and on April 10, 2002, Netanyahu spoke before the U.S. Senate, urging the United States to support Israel's fight against Palestinian terrorism. Netanyahu also is the author and editor of several books, including *International Terrorism: Challenge and Response* (1979) and *Terrorism: How the West Can Win* (1986).

Huey P. Newton

Huey P. Newton was born on February 17, 1942, to a poor family in Monroe, Louisiana, the youngest of seven children. His family moved to Oakland, California, in 1945. As a youth, Newton attended the Oakland public schools and was frequently suspended. While he was still a teenager, Newton was arrested for gun possession and vandalism. He supported himself in college by burglarizing homes in the Oakland and Berkeley Hills area. In 1964, at age twenty-two, he was convicted of assault with a deadly weapon and spent six months in the Alameda County jail, most of it in solitary confinement. After high school, Newton attended Merritt College and eventually earned an associate of arts degree. He later studied law at Oakland City College and at San Francisco Law School.

Newton's college experiences inspired an interest in politics and social issues. He became a member of the Afro-American Association, and he read books by revolutionaries such as Malcolm X, Chairman Mao Tse-tung, and Che Guevara. Also, Newton's lower class, African American background gave him an understanding of the evils of racial discrimination. In October 1966 Newton, along with Bobby Seale, organized the Black Panther Party for Self-Defense, an organization dedicated to defending the community against police aggression. Newton served as the group's minister of defense.

The Black Panther Party organized armed patrols to monitor the

Oakland police. Party members observed police procedure, advised citizens of their rights, tried to prevent abuse of citizens, and posted bail for those arrested. The group dressed in black, used slogans such as "power to the people," and gestures such as the raised, clenched fist to convey its opposition to oppression and its solidarity in the struggle to fight racism. Later, the group adopted a Maoist revolutionary ideology, and Newton and Seale wrote the Black Panther Party Platform and Program, which called for employment, housing, education, and exemption from military service for African Americans. Membership increased, and the party became the symbol of black struggle and pride.

The Federal Bureau of Investigation (FBI), along with the Central Intelligence Agency (CIA) and local police, actively targeted and eventually destroyed the Black Panther Party. In 1968 Newton was convicted of murdering Oakland police officer John Frey and was sentenced to fifteen years in prison. In May 1970, however, the California Appellate Court reversed Newton's conviction and ordered a new trial. Ultimately, the state of California dropped its case against Newton, citing technicalities, and Newton was released from prison. Thereafter, Newton changed the group's policies, abandoning its Marxist-Leninist views and concentrating on community programs, such as programs to provide food and education for children.

In 1974 Newton was charged with several assaults as well as the murder of a seventeen-year-old prostitute, Kathleen Smith. Newton failed to make his court appearance. He fled to Cuba, where he lived in exile for three years and worked as a machinist and a teacher. He came home in 1977 and was acquitted of the murder charges. Newton's troubles continued in 1985, when he was arrested for embezzling funds from the Black Panthers' community education and nutrition programs, and in 1989 he was convicted of embezzling funds from a school run by the group; he is said to have needed the money to support his alcohol and drug addictions. On August 22, 1989, Newton was gunned down by a drug dealer, ironically in the streets of Oakland where he grew up.

Muammar Qaddafi

Muammar Qaddafi was born in 1942 to a nomadic Bedouin family in Libya. At an early age, he is said to have planned coups to overthrow the colonial monarchy that ruled Libya. Qaddafi attended the University of Libya, graduating in 1964, and graduated from Libya's military academy in 1965, after which he became an army officer.

Throughout his time in the army, Qaddafi plotted the overthrow of the monarchy with a group of fellow officers. In 1969 he and his friends formed a secret revolutionary committee called the Free Officers Movement, and that same year they led a successful, bloodless military coup against King Idris. Qaddafi announced the coup over the radio on September 1, 1969, and proclaimed the creation of the Libyan Arab Republic. The monarchy had been aligned with Great Britain and the United States, and within months of the coup, Western troops were withdrawn as Qaddafi imposed an anti-Western, pro-Islam, Arab nationalist dictatorship in Libya.

After seizing power in 1969, Qaddafi nationalized foreign assets and used Libyan resources to promote his revolutionary socialist ideology throughout the world. He provided aid and supplies to various terrorist organizations and set up terrorist training camps in Libya. Groups receiving Libyan assistance included, for example, the Basques in Spain, the Sandinistas in Nicaragua, groups in El Salvador, the Irish Republican Army in Ireland, the Red Brigades in Italy, and others in Japan, Turkey, Thailand, and elsewhere, as well as the various Palestinian terrorist groups. In 1981 Qaddafi sent troops and weapons to aid the Palestine Liberation Organization (PLO) in the war in Lebanon.

Qaddafi also has been linked to direct terrorist acts committed by Libyan nationals. The most well-known incident occurred in December 1988, when a Pan American airliner blew up over Lockerbie, Scotland, killing 280 people. In November 1991 Britain and the United States announced that their investigation implicated two Libyan suspects in the bombing. The two suspects were indicted, and the United States demanded their extradition in order to stand trial in the United States. Qaddafi refused to turn over the Libyans, however, and in 1992 the United Nations imposed sanctions on air travel and arms sales to Libya. Finally, in 1999, Qaddafi handed over the two Libyan bombing suspects, and sanctions were suspended.

Since then, Qaddafi has sought to improve his relationship with Western European nations and has purportedly denounced terrorism. He has written a book called the *Green Book*, which is a treatise on his brand of Islamic socialism.

Ronald Reagan

Ronald Wilson Reagan was born on February 6, 1911, in Tampico, Illinois. He attended high school in nearby Dixon and then attended Eureka College, where he studied economics and sociology, played football, and acted in school plays. After his college graduation,

Reagan became a radio sports announcer. In 1937 Reagan took a screen test in Hollywood and began an acting career in which he appeared in fifty-three films over the next two decades. During this time, he married actress Jane Wyman and had two children, Maureen and Michael. In 1952 he married actress Nancy Davis and produced two more children, Patricia Ann and Ronald Prescott. Reagan also became president of the Screen Actors Guild, where he became involved in issues concerning communism in the film industry. His politics during this period became increasingly conservative.

In 1966 Reagan was elected governor of California by a margin of a million votes. He was reelected in 1970. In 1980 Reagan defeated Democratic incumbent president Jimmy Carter and became president of the United States. His vice president was Texas congressman George Bush. Reagan's victory can be credited in large part to voters' concerns about American hostages held in Iran since 1979.

Shortly after he took office, Reagan was shot by a would-be assassin, but his quick recovery increased his popularity among voters. In 1984 Reagan was reelected to a second term, defeating Democrat Walter F. Mondale. During his tenure as president, Reagan followed conservative policies of cutting taxes and increasing defense spending, leading to a large federal deficit. In foreign policy, Reagan improved relations with the Soviet Union and negotiated a treaty to eliminate intermediate-range nuclear missiles. In 1983 he ordered an invasion of the Caribbean island of Grenada, declaring that Americans there were in jeopardy and that the country had become a potentially dangerous Cuban-Soviet military base. Reagan also supported Iraq with large amounts of military aid during the Iran-Iraq War during the 1980s. Reagan's other long-standing foreign-policy initiative was to assist anti-Communist guerrillas, known as contras, in Nicaragua. The most damaging foreign-policy event of Reagan's presidency was the 1987 Iran-Contra Affair, in which the administration was found to have secretly sold arms to Iran in order to give the profits to the Nicaraguan contras; Reagan claimed he did not know of the diversion of monies.

Reagan also declared war against international terrorism. In a speech in 1985, Reagan denounced terrorism and the group of totalitarian countries that he said supported and trained terrorists, which he called "Murder, Incorporated." Terrorist incidents that occurred while Reagan was president included a 1983 attack by Hezbollah at a U.S. military base in Beirut, a 1985 hijacking of TWA Flight 847 to Beirut, a 1985 hijacking of Italian ocean liner *Achille Lauro*, and a 1986 attack by Libya on American soldiers in a West Berlin nightclub. Reagan's retaliation against Libya included several attacks by American planes on Libyan targets, including a 1986 attack on Tripoli, Libya's capital, which killed Libyan leader Muammar Qaddafi's daughter.

Maximilien Robespierre

Maximilien Robespierre (1758–1794) was born on May 6, 1758, in Arras, France. When he was six years old, his mother died; this disruption of his family life forced Robespierre to mature quickly and take on early responsibilities. At the age of eleven, he left home to attend the respected College of Louis-le-Grand and later the College of Law. He became a successful, admired lawyer and a gifted orator known for his stirring speeches. He was known as "the Incorruptible" for his honesty and moral virtues.

Early in his career, Robespierre supported the monarchy in France and was opposed to violence; he was devoted to the social theories of the French philosopher Jean Jacques Rousseau, a humanitarian who espoused values of human equality and belief in a divine deity. Ultimately, however, Robespierre became one of the most violent and influential figures of the French Revolution and the principal exponent of the Reign of Terror, a campaign of terror and atrocities that shocked the world.

Robespierre's involvement with the revolution came in 1789, when he was elected as a delegate to the Estates General, a group of representatives later called the National Assembly, formed to implement democratic reforms in the country. During his time with the assembly, Robespierre also participated in the Jacobin Club, a political club that provided an outlet for his speeches and political thoughts. The assembly removed King Louis XVI and Queen Marie Antoinette from the throne in 1792 and later beheaded them as traitors to France. On July 27, 1793, Robespierre was appointed to the twelve-member Committee of Public Safety, a body formed to govern the country. The committee, largely under Robespierre's leadership, took control of France at the height of the revolution. Robespierre, acting through the committee, proceeded to restore order to the country and protect the revolution from all enemies, both external and internal. This led to a terror campaign aimed at eliminating all persons who opposed the revolution—later called the Reign of Terror. The campaign, based on hearsay and often unfounded accusations, arrested and guillotined tens of thousands of civilians in France. Robespierre, once an inspiring leader, became a tyrant who sought to eliminate anyone who opposed his views.

Ironically, Robespierre died as a victim of his own terror campaign. After colleagues on the committee began to oppose his policies, Robespierre turned on them and they responded. On July 27, 1794, he was shot in the jaw and placed under arrest, and the following day he was executed on the guillotine.

George J. Tenet

George J. Tenet was born in New York State, is married to A. Stephanie Glakas-Tenet, and has one son, John Michael. He received a bachelor's degree from the Georgetown University School of Foreign Service in 1976 and a master's degree from the School of International Affairs at Columbia University in 1978.

Tenet began his Washington, D.C., political career working for Senator John Heinz as a legislative assistant and legislative director, covering issues such as national security and energy. In 1985 he began working for the Senate Select Committee on Intelligence as a designee to the vice chairman, Senator Patrick Leahy. In this position, Tenet directed the committee's oversight of all arms control negotiations between the Soviet Union and the United States, culminating in the preparation of a report to the U.S. Senate on the ability of U.S. intelligence to monitor the Intermediate Nuclear Force Treaty. In 1986 Tenet was appointed staff director of the committee, under the chairmanship of Senator David C. Boren. As staff director, he was responsible for coordinating all of the committee's oversight and legislative activities, including the strengthening of covert action reporting requirements, the creation of a statutory inspector general at the Central Intelligence Agency (CIA), and the introduction of comprehensive legislation to reorganize U.S. intelligence.

When President Bill Clinton was elected in 1992, Tenet served on the new administration's national security transition team and then was appointed special assistant to the president at the National Security Council (NSC). While at the NSC, he was the principal intelligence adviser to the national security adviser, coordinated various presidential decision directives on intelligence issues, and was responsible for coordinating all interagency activities concerning covert action.

In 1995 Tenet was appointed and confirmed as the deputy director of central intelligence; following the departure of CIA director John Deutch in December 1996, he served as acting director. On July 11, 1997, Tenet was sworn in as director of the CIA during Clinton's second term. As CIA director, Tenet heads the intelligence community (all foreign intelligence agencies of the United States) and directs the CIA. When Republican George W. Bush was elected in 2000, Bush asked Tenet to remain as CIA director, and he has continued in that role to the present day.

The September 11, 2001, terrorist attack clearly has provided Tenet and the CIA with many challenges. On February 6, 2002, Tenet assessed the current terrorist threat against the United States in Senate testimony, warning that Americans should expect future terrorist threats, possibly involving weapons of mass destruction.

Chronology

A.D. 66
A group of Jews in Judea called the Zealots, who are opposed to paying taxes to the Roman Empire, launches a terror campaign aimed at upper-class Jews who collaborated with the Romans.

1092
The Assassins, members of a minority Islamic sect, conduct suicide assassinations against the Turkish Ottoman Empire throughout the Middle East.

1792–1794
The French Revolution begins in France; King Louis XVI and Queen Marie-Antoinette are executed and the Committee of Public Safety is formed to govern the country, with Maximilien Robespierre as its leader; Robespierre uses a "Reign of Terror" to eliminate opposition to the revolution.

1876–1881
Anarchism, aimed at overthrowing tyrannical governments, becomes a popular political philosophy; one anarchist group, People's Will, forms in Russia with the goal of destroying the czarist government and giving power to workers; the group assassinates Czar Alexander II in 1881.

1886–1892
Prominent anarchists and organizers of a workers' protest set off a bomb, which kills police officers at Haymarket Square in Chicago in 1886; in 1892 anarchists Alexander Berkman and Emma Goldman conspire to bomb Carnegie Steel Company executive William Clay Frick in retaliation for the company's shooting workers during a labor strike.

1916–1923
A military revolt against British rule called the Easter Rising begins in Dublin, Ireland, in 1916; Irish rebels form a guer-

rilla group called the Irish Republican Army (IRA) to fight for Irish independence, with a political wing called Sinn Fein; the IRA begins a guerrilla campaign against British officers; in 1920 an incident called Bloody Sunday occurs in which British troops fire on a crowd watching a football match, killing twelve, in retaliation for the IRA's assassination of British intelligence officers; the parties sign the Anglo-Irish Treaty in 1921, giving most of southern, Catholic Ireland full independence, but preserving northern, mostly Protestant Ireland as a part of England; a civil war erupts in 1922 between those who supported the treaty with England and those who opposed it.

1917–1929
The October Revolution by the Bolsheviks in Russia begins, led by Lenin, and leads to a civil war, which the Bolsheviks win; Lenin dies in 1924 and is succeeded by Joseph Stalin, who implements his own campaign of terror to eliminate opposition to his rule.

1933–1945
Adolf Hitler becomes chancellor of Germany in 1933, quickly bans all parties but the Nazi Party, and creates a dictatorship with himself as the leader (Führer); Hitler begins military rearmament and a pattern of aggression toward neighboring states that leads to World War II; he also implements a program of genocide against the Jews and others; the Allies defeat the Germans in 1945, Hitler commits suicide, and shortly thereafter, the Nuremberg International Military Tribunal conducts a trial of the Nazi leaders for war crimes.

1934–1938
Stalin conducts the "Great Purge" in Russia, a wave of terror aimed at eliminating all opposition to his Communist, totalitarian rule.

1944–1948
Jews in Palestine form a terrorist group called Irgun to fight against British occupation and for a Jewish state; the group conducts numerous terrorist attacks, including a 1946 attack

on the King David Hotel, the headquarters of British military and civilian administration in Palestine, killing ninety-one and injuring forty-five, and a 1948 attack called the Deir Yassin massacre in which Irgun and others kill more than one hundred Palestinian civilians; in 1948 the British leave Palestine and the United Nations (UN) creates Israel as an independent Jewish state, dividing Palestine into separate Jewish and Palestinian areas.

1955–1962
Muslims in Algeria found the Front de Liberation Nationale (FLN) to fight for Algerian independence from French colonial rule; French prime minister Charles de Gaulle declares that Algerians have the right to self-determination; France negotiates with the FLN and a peace agreement is signed in 1962, leading to independence for Algeria.

1959–present
A terrorist group called Euskadi Ta Askatasuna (ETA) is formed in Spain to seek independence for Spain's Basque region, following repression by Spanish dictator General Francisco Franco; Franco dies in 1976, democracy is restored to Spain, and Spain grants autonomy to the Basque region; although a majority of the population is satisfied with these changes, the ETA has continued terrorist campaigns to the present day.

1960s–1970s
Left-wing revolutionary movements emerge in South America, including the Tupamaros in Uruguay, the National Liberation Action and the People's Revolutionary Vanguard in Brazil, the People's Revolutionary Army and the Montoneros in Argentina, the National Liberation Army in Bolivia, the Left Revolutionary Movement in Chile, the Revolutionary Armed Forces in Colombia, and the Shining Path in Peru.

1964–present
The Palestine Liberation Organization (PLO) is founded by Arab states in 1964; in 1967 the Six-Day War between Israelis and Arabs begins and Israel occupies Sinai and Gaza, the West

Bank, and the Golan Heights; in 1969 Yasser Arafat becomes the leader of the PLO and begins a prolonged campaign of terrorist strikes against the Israeli occupation of Palestine.

1966

Huey P. Newton and Bobby Seale found the Black Panther Party for Self-Defense, advocating armed struggle by blacks to fight racial discrimination and oppression in the United States.

1966–present

Fuerzas Armadas Revolucionarias de Colombia (FARC), the military wing of the Colombian Communist Party, is established in Colombia and begins a four-decades-long guerrilla war against the right-wing Colombian government; FARC receives funding from Colombia's drug trade and conducts terrorist strikes on political targets up to the present day.

1969–1999

In Libya, Muammar Qaddafi successfully overthrows the monarchy in 1969 and proclaims the Libyan Arab Republic; following the coup, British and U.S. troops withdraw from Libya and, throughout the 1970s and 1980s, Libya supports various terrorist groups and conducts its own terrorism against the United States and Western targets, including a 1986 bomb in a Berlin discotheque that kills an American soldier, a 1988 bombing of Pan Am Flight 103 over Lockerbie, Scotland, killing 270 people, and a 1989 bombing of a French airliner (UTA Flight 772) over the Sahara Desert; in 1992 the United Nations imposes economic sanctions on Libya for its refusal to hand over the Lockerbie suspects; in 1999 Libya finally hands over Abdel Basset Ali al-Megrahi and Lamen Khalifa Fhimah to the United Nations and the UN sanctions against Libya are suspended.

1970s

European left-wing terrorist groups with the goal of fighting capitalism emerge; these groups include the Red Brigades, which forms in Italy and carries out bombings, kidnappings, and murders designed to paralyze the Italian government, and the Red Army (or Baader-Meinhof Gang), which conducts a similar campaign in Germany.

1970s–1990s

In the 1970s and 1980s, a period known as the Troubles occurs in Northern Ireland, characterized by numerous terrorist strikes by the Irish Republican Army against British and Protestant targets; on January 30, 1972, now known as Bloody Friday, in response to the British shooting of unarmed demonstrators, the IRA detonates twenty-six car bombs within forty minutes in Belfast, killing eleven and injuring 130 people; thereafter, the Northern Ireland Parliament (Stormont) is suspended and direct rule from Britain is imposed; in the late 1970s the IRA conducts a bombing campaign against the British government; in March 1981 Republican prisoners in British jails stage a hunger strike, led by prisoner Bobby Sands, to protest British policy in Northern Ireland; on October 12, 1984, the IRA detonates a bomb at the Grand Hotel in Brighton, England, killing five and almost killing British prime minister Margaret Thatcher; in 1985 Britain begins negotiations with the Irish Republic government, resulting in the November 12, 1985, Anglo-Irish agreement; the agreement is protested by the Unionists in Northern Ireland, and violence from both Unionists and Republicans continues in the 1980s; in 1997 the IRA declares a cease-fire; in 1998 a peace agreement is reached that paves the way for a power-sharing government in Northern Ireland, improving chances for peace.

1970s–present

Two radical Islamist terrorist groups form in Egypt, Jamaat al-Islamiyya and the Egyptian Islamic Jihad; both groups seek to overthrow the secular government in Egypt and install an Islamic government; Egypt successfully stops most terrorist activity by these groups within Egypt during the 1990s, but the Islamic Jihad operates today in exile and leaders from both groups have strong ties to al-Qaeda and Osama bin Laden.

1972

The Black September terrorist group, affiliated with the PLO, kills eleven Israeli athletes at the Olympic Games in Munich, Germany.

1974

The Weather Underground, a domestic terrorist group in the United States, releases a statement called "Prairie Fire" that sets forth its plan for armed struggle against the Vietnam War; thereafter, the group sets off numerous bombs in U.S. government facilities in the 1970s.

1979–1981

The Islamic Revolution begins in Iran in 1979, led by Ayatollah Khomeini; thereafter, Iran becomes a state that supports terrorism; on November 4, 1979, Iranian students seize the American embassy in Tehran to protest the U.S. admission of the ex-shah of Iran for medical treatment; fifty-two American hostages are held for 444 days, until their release is negotiated on January 20, 1981.

1980s

Two revolutionary terrorist groups in Peru take up arms, the Shining Path, a militant Maoist group (founded in 1970) that seeks a peasant revolution, and Tupac Amaru, a Marxist group that wants to install a Communist government.

1980s–1990s

Between 1980 and 1987, Iraq fights a war with Iran, receives Western military aid, and develops into a strong military power; Iraq uses chemical weapons against Iran during the war and on its own Kurdish population, gives support to terrorist groups, and begins to develop weapons of mass destruction; in 1990 Iraq invades Kuwait, leading to a U.S. military assault, weapons inspections lasting until 1998 (which were reinstated in 2002), and economic sanctions that remain in place.

1981

On October 6, the Islamic Jihad assassinates Egyptian president Anwar Sadat.

1982–1984

The Israelis stage a massive invasion of Lebanon in 1982 to fight the PLO; UN Security Council Resolution 509 demands that Israel withdraw all its military forces, but Israel advances rapidly to Beirut and massacres hundreds of Palestinian civilians in the Lebanese Palestinian refugee camps of Sabra and Shatilla; the terrorist group Hezbollah is founded in 1982 in Lebanon by Shiite Arabs linked with Iran's Islamic Revolution to fight Israel's occupation of Lebanon; Hezbollah makes a series of terrorist strikes against Israeli and U.S. targets, and both Israel and the United States withdraw from Lebanon in the next several years.

1983

April 18: A Hezbollah suicide bomber destroys the American embassy in Beirut, killing sixty people.

October 23: A Hezbollah suicide bomber strikes the U.S. marine compound in Beirut, killing 245 marines and fifty-eight French paratroopers.

1984

April: Eighteen U.S. servicemen die in an attack by Hezbollah launched at a U.S. air base in Spain.

September 20: A car bomb attack by Hezbollah kills twenty-four, including two American servicemen, at the U.S. embassy in Lebanon.

December 12: The Islamic Jihad bombs the U.S. and French embassies in Kuwait, a U.S. housing compound, a Kuwaiti oil field, an airline terminal, and a Kuwaiti government office.

1987

December: Palestinians in the West Bank and Gaza rise up in a popular civil revolt against Israeli occupation named "Intifada" (Arabic for "shaking off"); the Intifada is supported by the PLO and leads to the formation of several Islamic terrorist groups opposed to the secular PLO leadership, groups such as Hamas and the Palestinian Islamic Jihad.

1988
Osama bin Laden establishes al-Qaeda, an organization of ex-mujahideen, to aid the Afghan resistance against the Soviets in Afghanistan.

1989
June: The National Islamic Front overthrows the elected government of Prime Minister Sadiq al-Mahdi of Sudan in a military coup, creating a fundamentalist Islamic government in Sudan that supports various Islamic terrorist groups.

1990s
The fundamentalist Islamic group al-Qaeda, led by bin Laden, begins a terror campaign aimed at the United States and conducts a number of terrorist attacks on American targets.

1991–present
The Soviet Union collapses in 1991, and the Chechens, a fundamentalist Islamic ethnic group in the Caucasus region of Russia, begin a terrorist campaign aimed at winning independence; the group fights two wars with Russia in Chechnya, and the conflict continues to the present day.

1992
December 29: A bombing at the Gold Mohur Hotel in Yemen kills two and wounds four tourists (but the bomb fails to hit one hundred American servicemen in the area).

1992–present
In 1992, Algeria voids the victory of the Islamic Salvation Front (FIS), the largest Islamic opposition party, in the first round of legislative elections; radical Islamists form the Armed Islamic Group, known by its French acronym, GIA, to overthrow the secular Algerian government and replace it with an Islamic state; the terrorist group is responsible for terrorist attacks in France and attacks on Algerian civilians, including two bombings in Algiers in August 2001.

1992–present
Israel elects Labor Party leader Yitzhak Rabin as prime min-

ister in 1992 and begins peace negotiations with Yasser Arafat, leader of the PLO; on September 13, 1993, the two sides sign the Oslo Accords, providing for Palestinian self-rule; Arafat is later elected leader of the Palestinians; over the next several years, Israel withdraws from certain areas of Palestine, but the West Bank and Gaza Strip remain under Israeli control, Israel does not dismantle any settlements, and the number of settlers and new settlements increases considerably; Palestinian groups during this period continue terrorist activities; on November 3, 1995, Rabin is assassinated by a Jewish right-wing extremist; the peace process fails, and the PLO-Israel conflict continues to the present day.

1993
February 26: The first bombing of the World Trade Center in New York City kills six and injures more than one thousand (Ramzi Yousef, who has links to al-Qaeda, is later convicted of the crime).

October 3–4: Bin Laden claims that he supplied weapons and fighters to Somalis involved in a fierce battle that left eighteen U.S. servicemen dead in Mogadishu, Somalia.

1995
March 20: The Aum Shinrikyo religious cult in Japan attacks civilians on a subway using sarin gas, a deadly nerve agent, killing five and injuring more than five thousand.

April 19: A car bomb destroys the Murrah Federal Building in Oklahoma City, Oklahoma; Timothy McVeigh, a right-wing ex-soldier, is later convicted and executed for this crime.

November 13: A car bomb at a U.S.-run training facility in Saudi Arabia for the Saudi National Guard kills five Americans and two Indians.

1996
June 25: A truck bomb at the Khobar Towers apartment compound in Dhahran, Saudi Arabia, where hundreds of U.S. Air Force personnel are stationed, kills nineteen U.S. airmen and wounds hundreds more.

July 27: A pipe bomb kills one person and wounds 111 at the Olympic Games in Atlanta, Georgia.

1998
February: Bin Laden issues a joint declaration with other Islamic terrorist groups under the banner of the "World Islamic Front," stating that Muslims should kill Americans, including civilians, anywhere in the world.

May: Theodore Kaczynski, known as the "Unabomber," is sentenced to life imprisonment for an eighteen-year campaign of mail bombings in the United States that killed three people and injured twenty-three others.

August 7: Truck bombs hit U.S. embassies in Tanzania and Kenya, killing 224, including twelve Americans (in 2001, four terrorists are convicted of this crime).

2000
August 12: A boat containing explosives rams the USS *Cole* in Yemen, killing seventeen sailors and wounding more than thirty; the attack is attributed to al-Qaeda.

2000–present
September 28: On September 28, 2000, Israeli opposition leader Ariel Sharon visits the Temple Mount, a Muslim holy site in Jerusalem, marking the beginning of the second Palestinian Intifada against Israel and leading to numerous terrorist attacks on Israeli targets by militant Palestinian groups; Sharon is elected prime minister of Israel in 2001, and in March 2002, in response to the increased terrorist suicide attacks on Israeli civilians, he mounts Operation "Defensive Wall" in the West Bank, arrests Palestinian leaders, and imprisons Arafat in his compound in Ramallah; the Palestinian/Israeli conflict continues to the present day, with numerous Palestinian terrorist attacks on Israeli civilians and retaliatory strikes by Israel against Palestinian-controlled areas.

2001
May 27: Abu Sayyaf, a Philippines-based radical Islamic terrorist group, kidnaps twenty people, including three Ameri-

cans, at a Philippine resort and demands ransom payments; ultimately, one of the Americans is killed, and the other two—a Christian missionary couple—are held hostage until a 2002 rescue attempt results in the killing of one hostage and the release of the other.

September 11: Four passenger airliners hijacked by al-Qaeda terrorists crash into New York City's World Trade Center, the Pentagon, and a field in rural Pennsylvania, killing thousands; shortly thereafter, on September 20, U.S. president George Bush declares a "War on Terror," and on October 7, the United States and its allies begin a military attack on the Taliban regime in Afghanistan and al-Qaeda terrorists worldwide.

2002
January 29: Bush declares an "axis of evil," referring to countries that support terror and seek weapons of mass destruction (specifically identifying Iraq, Iran, and North Korea); Bush later threatens unilateral action against Iraq and seeks the United Nations's help to return weapons inspectors to Iraq.

February 23: FARC forces in Colombia kidnap presidential candidate Ingrid Betancourt, a vocal critic of FARC's failure to make peace and its connection with the Colombian drug trade.

March 27: Hamas takes responsibility for a suicide bombing that kills twenty-eight and injures 140 Israelis at a Passover seder.

September 24: A bombing by the Basque separatist group ETA kills a civil guard and wounds three others in Spain.

October–December: On October 4, North Korea admits to developing nuclear weapons, and during December proceeds to reopen a sealed plutonium reprocessing plant, disable surveillance cameras, and expel UN weapons inspectors; the United States pursues diplomatic efforts to persuade the country to abandon its nuclear efforts.

October 12: A tourist resort in Bali is bombed by a terrorist group, Jemaah Islamiyah, believed to be linked to al-Qaeda.

October 14: Britain suspends a power-sharing agreement in

Northern Ireland after Sinn Fein officials are linked to continued IRA military activity in raids conducted on October 4.

October 23: Chechen rebels seize a theater in Moscow, taking hundreds of civilians hostage and demanding that Russia end its war in Chechnya; the Russian response to the theater takeover is to storm the theater with gas weapons, an action that kills the rebels, as well as more than one hundred hostages.

November 28: Terrorists linked with al-Qaeda strike Israeli targets in Kenya, bombing a hotel, killing ten Kenyans and three Israelis, and failing in an attempt to shoot down an Israeli charter plane using modern antiaircraft weaponry.

December 28: Chechen suicide bombers blow up the headquarters of Chechnya's pro-Russian government in Grozny, Chechnya, killing forty-six and wounding many more.

For Further Research

Books

YONAH ALEXANDER AND MICHAEL S. SWETNAM, *Usama bin Laden's al-Qaida: Profile of a Terrorist Network.* Ardsley, NY: Transnational Publishers, 2001.

MENACHEM BEGIN, *The Revolt.* New York: Nash, 1977.

PETER L. BERGEN, *Holy War: Inside the Secret World of Osama bin Laden.* New York: Free Press, 2001.

RICHARD BERNSTEIN, *Out of the Blue: The Story of September 11, 2001, from Jihad to Ground Zero.* New York: Henry Holt, 2002.

YOSSEF BODANSKY, *Bin Laden: The Man Who Declared War on America.* Rocklin, CA: Forum, 1999.

RICHARD BUTLER, *The Greatest Threat.* New York: Public-Affairs, 2000.

CALEB CARR, *The Lessons of Terror, a History of Warfare Against Civilians: Why It Has Always Failed and Why It Will Fail Again.* New York: Random House, 2002.

JOHN K. COOLEY, *Unholy Wars: Afghanistan, America, and International Terrorism.* 2nd ed. London: Pluto Press, 2000.

ISAAC CRONIN, *Confronting Fear: A History of Terrorism.* New York: Thunder's Mouth Press, 2002.

SIMHA FLAPAN, *The Birth of Israel: Myths and Realities.* New York: Pantheon Books, 1987.

PAUL HALSALL, ED., *Modern History Sourcebook.* New York: Fordham University, 1998.

PHILIP B. HEYMANN, *Terrorism and America: A Common-sense Strategy for a Democratic Society.* Cambridge, MA: MIT Press, 1998.

BRUCE HOFFMAN, *Inside Terrorism*. New York: Columbia University Press, 1998.

JAMES F. HOGE JR. AND GIDEON ROSE, EDS., *How Did This Happen?* New York: PublicAffairs, 2001.

FEREYDOUN HOVEYDA, *The Broken Crescent: The "Threat" of Militant Islamic Fundamentalism.* Westport, CT: Praeger, 1998.

DAVID JOHN CAWDELL IRVING, *The War Path: Hitler's Germany, 1933–1939.* London: Joseph, 1978.

HALA JABER, *Hezbollah: Born with a Vengeance.* New York: Columbia University Press, 1997.

WALTER LAQUEUR, *The New Terrorism: Fanaticism and the Arms of Mass Destruction.* New York: Oxford University Press, 1999.

WALTER LAQUEUR AND YONAH ALEXANDER, EDS., *The Terrorism Reader.* New York: NAL Penguin, 1987.

SANDRA MACKEY, *The Reckoning: Iraq and the Legacy of Saddam Hussein.* New York: W.W. Norton, 2002.

PHEBE MARR, *Iraq, Troubles, and Tension: Persian Gulf Futures I.* Washington, DC: National Defense University, Institute for National Strategic Studies, 1997.

AHMAD MAWSILILI, *Historical Dictionary of Islamic Fundamentalist Movements in the Arab World, Iran, and Turkey.* Lanham, MD: Scarecrow Press, 1999.

HUEY P. NEWTON, *To Die for the People.* New York: Random House, 1972.

EDGAR O'BALLANCE, *Islamic Fundamentalist Terrorism, 1979–1995: The Iranian Connection.* New York: New York University Press, 1997.

ALBERT PARRY, *Terrorism: From Robespierre to Arafat.* New York: Vanguard Press, 1976.

SCOTT RITTER, *Endgame: Solving the Iraq Problem—Once and for All.* New York: Simon and Schuster, 1999.

Avi Shlaim, *The Iron Wall: Israel and the Arab World.* New York: W.W. Norton, 2000.

Periodicals

Khalid Amayreh, "Hizbullah vs. Arafat," *Middle East International,* June 2, 2000.

Associated Press, "Baghdad Says U.S. Is 'Lying' About Iraqi Weapons Program," *New York Times,* August 12, 2002.

Peter Beinart, "War Paths," *New Republic,* February 18, 2002.

Nicholas Blanford, "Hizbollah Opens Its Doors to All," *Middle East,* December 1997.

Harold Brackman, "Going It Alone Against International Evil," *Midstream,* May/June 2002.

Daniel Byman, "The Rollback Fantasy: Using the Iraqi Opposition to Oust Saddam Hussein Would Lead to a Replay of the Bay of Pigs," *Foreign Affairs,* January/February 1999.

Charles A. Duelfer, "Why Iraq Will Never Give Up Its Worst Weapons," *Aviation Week and Space Technology,* March 11, 2002.

Gregg Easterbrook, "The Big One: The Real Danger Is Nuclear," *New Republic,* November 5, 2001.

Economist, "Know Thine Enemy: Weapons Proliferation," February 2, 2002.

Mitch Frank, "Osama's World," *Time,* September 24, 2001.

Neve Gordon, "Defining Terrorism, and Assigning the Label," *National Catholic Reporter,* April 4, 1997.

Brian Michael Jenkins, "Terrorism and Beyond: A 21st Century Perspective," *Studies in Conflict and Terrorism,* September/October 2001.

PHILIP JENKINS, "Home-Grown Terror," *American Heritage*, September 1995.

GEORGE JOHNSON, "Order of Magnitude: The Toll and the Technology," *New York Times*, September 16, 2001.

JOSEPH KAHN, "A Trend Toward Attacks That Emphasize Deaths," *New York Times*, September 12, 2001.

ELIE KEDOURIE, "Political Terror in the Muslim World," *Encounter*, February 1987.

JAMES KITFIELD, "Osama's Learning Curve," *National Journal*, November 10, 2001.

DAVID LENNON, "The UK's Long Terror Experience," *Europe*, October 2001.

RICHARD MACKENZIE, "The Succession: The Price of Neglecting Afghanistan," *New Republic*, September 14, 1998.

JOSHUA MICAH MARSHALL, "Bomb Saddam?" *Washington Monthly*, June 2002.

JUDITH MILLER, "Iraqi Tells of Renovations at Sites for Chemical and Nuclear Arms," *New York Times*, December 20, 2001.

KENNETH M. POLLACK, "Iraq and the United States: Ready for War," *Foreign Affairs*, March/April 2002.

DAVID C. RAPOPORT, "The Fourth Wave: September 11 in the History of Terrorism," *Current History*, December 2001.

JEREMY SALT, "Armageddon in the Middle East?" *Arena Magazine*, April/May 2002.

MICHAEL SATCHELL, "Complacent No More," *U.S. News & World Report*, September 14, 2001.

JONATHAN B. TUCKER, "Historical Trends Related to Bioterrorism: An Empirical Analysis," *Emerging Infectious Diseases*, July/August 1999.

AL J. VENTER, "How Saddam Almost Built His Bomb," *Middle East Policy*, February 1999.

MARTIN WALKER, "A Brief History of Terrorism," *Europe*, October 2001.

STEPHEN ZUNES, "Confrontation with Iraq: A Bankrupt U.S. Policy," *Middle East Policy*, June 1998.

Websites

COUNCIL ON FOREIGN RELATIONS, Terrorism: Questions and Answers, www.terrorismanswers.com. The council is nonpartisan membership organization, research center, and publisher of *Foreign Relations* that is dedicated to increasing America's understanding of the world and contributing ideas to U.S. foreign policy.

DEPARTMENT OF HOMELAND SECURITY, www.whitehouse.gov/homeland. The official site for the Department of Homeland Security.

ILLINOIS INSTITUTE OF TECHNOLOGY, PAUL V. GALVIN LIBRARY, Government Publications Access, www.gl.iit.edu/govdocs/terrorism.htm. This site makes available official documents of the United States and international governments concerning terrorism.

NATIONAL SECURITY ARCHIVE, www.gwu.edu/~nsarchiv. This is a nonprofit research institute on international affairs that has a library and an archive of declassified U.S. documents obtained through the Freedom of Information Act. It also indexes and publishes documents in book, microfiche, and electronic formats.

U.S. CENTRAL INTELLIGENCE AGENCY, The War on Terrorism, www.cia.gov/terrorism/index.html. A government website providing information about the War on Terror and terrorism.

U.S. DEPARTMENT OF STATE, Response to Terrorism, http://usinfo.state.gov/topical/pol/terror. A government website providing news and information about terrorism and issues of international security.

Index